360 Degree Appraisal

Financial Times Management Briefings are happy to receive proposals from individuals who have expertise in the field of management education.

If you would like to discuss your ideas further, please contact Andrew Mould, Commissioning Editor.

Tel: 0171 447 2210
Fax: 0171 240 5771
e-mail: andrew.mould@pitmanpub.co.uk

FINANCIAL TIMES

Management Briefings

360 Degree Appraisal

NICHOLAS BAHRA

FT
PITMAN
PUBLISHING

London · Hong Kong · Johannesburg · Melbourne · Singapore · Washington DC

Human Resources

PITMAN PUBLISHING
128 Long Acre, London WC2E 9AN
Tel: +44 (0)171 447 2000
Fax: +44 (0)171 240 5771

A Division of Pearson Professional Limited

First published in Great Britain 1997

ISBN 0 273 63170 5

British Library Cataloguing in Publication Data
A CIP catalogue record for this book can be obtained from the British Library.

10 9 8 7 6 5 4 3 2 1

Printed and bound in Great Britain

The Publishers' policy is to use paper manufactured from sustainable forests.

Contents

Note

This best practice guide has been written to help you to introduce a 360 degree appraisal system into your organisation. It is designed to assist and guide you without assumptions or knowledge of your own particular goals or remit. Therefore, it is strongly recommended that you seek advice from someone who has direct experience of implementing 360 degree appraisal if possible.

Preface

During this century, Henry Ford started a company, Sir John Harvey Jones expanded one, Bill Gates surprised a few and so did Robert Maxwell. This century has seen economic change and human warfare on perhaps a different global scale than before. The way people have chosen to recruit and train people has also played its part. Arguably, we now have more management specialists and gurus, more techniques and methodologies, more collected information and collective knowledge than ever before about the way people behave and perform at work.

360 degree appraisal and its associated processes puts the assessment and development of people where it firmly belongs – with the people that are able to tell the difference between those who make a positive contribution and those who do not. Many appraisal systems in the past have, on occasions, become trivialised and may not have assisted the individuals or the organisations for which they were designed.

This has been because the people responsible for the planning, design, implementation and evaluation of appraisal systems saw problems and issues associated with staff development or performance as being generally between manager and subordinate. In an attempt to raise awareness of issues and to clarify what people were saying and agreeing to do, there has also been a tendency for practitioners to be concerned about what looked right and acceptable on paper for senior management. Herein lies the problem.

This is not a criticism of bureaucracy, as often it can be critical for staff appraisals to 'look right' on paper to achieve the desired result. However, the evaluation of most initiatives is cloudy to say the least with 'external factors or other influences' usually to blame if the initiative undertaken does not deliver what it promised. One assumption that is made during the writing of this report is that any professional individual today needs to demonstrate how they contribute to the success of the organisation which they are working for or associated with. One way by which this may be measured is by the level of willingness to assist their colleagues to also succeed.

'Ownership' of staff development has been debated for many years and varies from company to company depending on its culture, growth phase, environment and many other factors. Arguably, one of the most significant influences as to whose responsibility it is to ensure there are adequate and proper systems, plus structures and methods for staff development, is the senior management team or directors of the organisation.

Therefore, in organisations today, the most senior person from management needs to be involved with any process such as 360 degree appraisal in order for it to be effective. Otherwise – and this may come as a surprise for some – the company will have wasted a significant proportion of its spend on this process. It may look good for a while and its effect may appear to be considerable in the short term; however, its real impact will be very different from what is perceived.

So, in the essence of good practice, it will be necessary to include the involvement of the most senior of personnel. If senior management do not support, assist and participate willingly in the process of 360 degree appraisal, this methodology cannot prove to be really effective and it is strongly recommended that it is not implemented.

The author can be contacted through the publishers.

Why you need to read this report

For any professional individual working in a public or private organisation today, 360 degree appraisal could be part of your working routine soon if it has not already become so. Yet to implement 360 degree appraisal successfully, you will need to acquire knowledge and expertise in a specialist area of human resource development, which is a generic term for personnel management or training.

If you acquire this fundamental knowledge, you will be able to influence the success of your own personal development and of those around you. In short, you will add value to both you and your colleagues. Translated into something tangible, it could mean that you will become more valuable or employable.

Common processes used by companies to assess their people:

- an interview

- a structured interview

- ability tests

- personality measures

- psychometric assessments

- staff appraisal

- past performance track record

- academic performance.

What this report is about

This best practice report will focus on the last two points listed below: how an individual assesses themselves and how they are assessed by others. This is more than a person's reputation in the eyes of their colleagues. Indeed, it attempts to dissuade such superficial and judgemental methods which often prevail during an individual's recruitment, selection, training, promotion and sometimes termination, at great cost in human and financial terms. 360 degree appraisal and its associated methods can provide an objective way to assess an individual's performance in a number of critical and non-critical areas.

Often, the focus of assessment is to determine the following:

- what the person can do

- the amount of work they can do

- the quality of their work

- their skill ownership

- their marketability

- their employability

- what they contribute to the task

- what they contribute to the team

- what they contribute to the organisation

- what they contribute to society

- how the individual sees the organisation

- how the individual assesses their own performance

- how the individual assesses the performance of others.

1 Assessment

1.1 Introduction to Assessment

If anyone claims to have invented 360 degree appraisal, don't believe them. As a methodology, similar to 'competencies' or 'appraisals', its derivations are probably centuries old. Firstly, I think it is important to realise that 360 degree appraisal is a form of assessment process or system. This means that people need to understand and demonstrate personal competency in assessing other people. It seems rather easy, yet in practice it may prove to be a disaster.

For example, if you were asked for the first time to assess the capability of the astronaut Buzz Aldrin, all former prime ministers of the UK or Roald Dahl the story-teller, how would you actually do this? Presumably it would be difficult to know by which criteria the individual should be assessed. The added complication might be that unless you had worked for a reasonable period of time with any of these individuals, how would you assess their abilities, personality or workstyle? Would you base it on what you read in the media, or perhaps by their reputation?

In fact, to understand how to use 360 degree appraisal well, it is critical to have, at the very least, an appreciation of the real meaning of assessment. During the last 4,000 years, we have tried to establish methods to introduce objectivity to the assessment process and the first recorded reference to the use of assessment was in Asia around 2200 BC. Since then, the sophistication and use of language has enabled us to devise ever more complex methods of verbal questioning. Also there has been a much greater interest in the development of written questionnaires.

Professional Psychology

Everybody is an amateur psychologist. That is to say, everyone uses their senses and thoughts to analyse human behaviour. Some people do this more consciously than others and some appear to be more 'expert' than others. In the UK we have a range of professional providers of psychological test or assessment materials which have undergone extensive research to assess what they can actually predict (or not) about a person's behaviour. There are also a number of professional psychologists with varying degrees of qualifications.

Qualifications

This is a confusing area. Currently, there is no official accreditation programme, yet there are 'chartered' psychologists and 'registered test users' who hold certificates of competence. As it is generally the process of administration and interpretation of a personality or psychological test which is critical to its 'best practice' use, you are advised to check the certification or status of anyone saying they are a psychologist.

Currently there is no legislation to stop anyone from saying they are a psychologist, which is rather strange considering the professionalism which prevails in the industry. To give you a particularly simplistic yet relevant analogy, there are good and bad plumbers, accountants and doctors and the same applies to psychologists. One of the easiest places to check the credentials of a practitioner or consultant is to call the British Psychological Society (see addresses at the end).

Some practitioners have studied for up to eight years to acquire the status of 'chartered' psychologist and typically will have a first degree in psychology, a Masters in behavioural science and will have demonstrated personal competence during their field work under supervision. You will also find a range of consultants who have many years direct experience of people development and also have certificates to assess people using personality measures or instruments.

Quality

If you wish to check the quality of a psychologist's work, try speaking with someone who has recently employed them. Also find out if they have published anything academically recently or who their clients have been over a period of years and whether or not their input at the time made a positive difference to the organisation. This whole area needs more clarity for the buyers of professional psychological services. As the profession evolves and refines its theories and concepts, it will be better able to provide practical solutions for business, if the opportunities are made available. This is a difficult area as the equation will always be value for money, and despite the efforts of companies to link this type of service to the bottom line, few firms will actually spend sufficient time analysing this part of the evaluation process.

Psychological Testing

This section is to provide you with some guidance about test procedures in the UK. The reason you will need to know a little about testing before you implement 360 degree appraisal is because:

- if not properly administered, any results derived from 360 degree appraisal will have little meaning;

- you may be administering or using a psychological test and will need to know your personal liability as a test user.

Whether or not 360 degree appraisal is a 'test' is debatable. Psychological tests are designed to provide partial assessment of certain attributes. These are general intellectual ability, specific capacities or aptitudes, interests or personality. The usefulness of a test depends on its being well designed, properly administered and correctly interpreted. Outcomes will nearly always be dependent on the context of the other relevant information about the person being tested.

Below are two definitions reproduced from *Psychological Testing*, a guide recently produced by the British Psychological Society:

> A psychological test is an instrument designed to produce a quantitative assessment of some psychological attribute or attributes.
>
> A psychological test is any procedure on the basis of which inferences are made concerning a person's capacity, propensity or liability to act, react, experience, or to structure or order thought or behaviour in particular ways.

What This Means

The crucial elements are these. First of all a test is a procedure. This means that there will be a predetermined task, activity or series of questions. The other point of major significance is that the procedure will provide the basis for inference. How satisfactory the basis for inference is and to what extent, is usually the focus for discussion about the quality of tests.

Also, you will find the inferences drawn will be related to psychological importance. So, for example, a colour vision test or a test of manual dexterity are physical assessments, whereas to assess an individual's behaviour in the workplace would strictly speaking be a psychological assessment.

Technically, if professional judgement is formed on the basis of observation and extended questioning, for instance in a court of law, then there is no test although inferences may be drawn. If no inferences are drawn, then clearly this will be a reporting of events rather than a test.

What is a Test?

What makes a test a test is that users appeal to its qualities in support of their judgement or recommendations. The procedure lends credence to the inference, the inference depends on the quality of the procedure. In short, a test is a portable aid to decision-making.

The Range of Tests Available

Testing procedures vary in the degree of complexity of their administration, scoring and interpretation. There are over 4,500 published tests available today.

What These Tests Measure

Typically, these tests or assessments evaluate different facets of individual behaviour. This is achieved by a standard set of questions and the scores are then calculated against statistical data which has been collated and analysed over the years. So far, the questionnaires mentioned have been psychological or personality based and can be used as a predictor of likely job success.

Other Forms of Tests

Apart from personality measures, there are also measures of maximum performance. These types of measures look at how accurate and quickly people can do things, or how much they know and how great their potential is. Examples are:

•   general ability tests

•   work sampling tests

•   aptitude tests

- numeric ability tests

- language ability tests.

Interest and Preference Measures

These types of questionnaires are specifically designed to measure an individual's likes and dislikes for different types of work in a systematic manner. They may be developed from a theory as to why people have preferences for certain types of job, or they may have been developed through rigourous statistical analysis for the link between the questions and particular performances.

Reliability and Validity

A good test will have undergone extensive research by suitably qualified academics which will assess its reliability and validity. Complex statistical modelling will be used along with techniques such as test and re-test validity which will look at an individual's scores over a period of time. Particular studies may, for example, look at similar groups of people. These groups could be scientists, sales people, managing directors of multinationals, cleaners or security guards.

Do Not Assume That All Tests Are Equally Reliable

Anyone may write a test. The trend recently has been for psychologists to write tailor-made questionnaires or to produce assessments which may be easily tailored to clients' needs. A good test will normally provide data and information by which to validate its research. Reputable test publishers, such as those listed with the British Psychological Society, will be able and willing to provide such information on request if you are a prospective client. If you are thinking of purchasing test materials from any of those listed or others which are not, you are advised to ask for this type of information to satisfy yourself that sufficient research has been carried out.

If you have not purchased test material before, you are advised to spend some time researching the market. None of these tests can lay claim to replacing a traditional interview, but they will be used as part of a structured process to assist the professional recruiter, manager or trainer. In 1996, virtually all firms in the UK Times Top 1000 use some form of questionnaire (personality or ability) to assist with staff recruitment, selection or training.

The Last Century

The National Institute of Industrial Psychology was founded in London in 1921. In 1928, a similar body was set up in France. Also in the 1900s there were breakthroughs in the development of the first group of intelligence questionnaires for US Army recruits. The period between 1925 and 1950 saw the spread of standardised questioning and the development of a methodology and technology for questioning. During the Second World War, William C. Shutz PhD developed an interesting theory. His suggestion was that the gunners on US Navy battleships had better performance levels when they were more comfortable with each other as team members and had built up a kind of rapport with each other's personality.

Shutz developed a test today known as 'FIRO-B'. Its full title is Fundamental Interpersonal Relations Orientation – Behaviour. From a series of 54 carefully constructed questions, Shutz was able to compile a personality profile of the individual. This profile which gave an individual ratings on a scale of 0–9 on three dimensions of interpersonal relationships (Inclusion, Control and Affection) was found to be helpful to the individual in terms of understanding their own personality and also helpful to others when they compared their profiles.

What 54 Questions Measure

Some people found they were more likely to need the company of other people and others preferred to remain alone. Some needed to control events and others preferred to be controlled. Some needed praise, encouragement and recognition for their work and others did not. These three statements are extremely simplistic examples of what may be discovered through the use of FIRO-B. With professional administration and interpretation, a great deal of insight and information can be gained about observable and less directly observable behaviour to assist in understanding and predicting a person's behaviour.

Other Questionnaires

Another questionnaire is the 'Sixteen Personality Factor Questionnaire', or 16 PF, which was first published in 1949 by IPAT (Institute for Personality and Ability Testing Inc.). This questionnaire has been widely used in clinical, educational and occupational contexts to provide information for psychologists and professional practitioners such as trainers and consultants, and to ease decision-making about people. Originally devised by Raymond

B. Cattell and assisted by numerous researchers, including Dr. Samuel Krug, this questionnaire is a multidimensional set of sixteen questionnaire scales, arranged in omnibus form.

The 16 PF has between 105 and 187 questions (psychologists call them items) and has seven different versions. Its publication was undertaken to meet a demand from research psychologists for a personality-measuring instrument, duly validated with respect to the primary personality factors and rooted in the basic concepts of general psychology. In the UK the research was pioneered by the late Frank Warburton and the questionnaire has been correlated with other questionnaires (or instruments) and will provide measures on scales including the following personality traits:

- Reserved or Warmhearted

- Humble or Assertive

- Practical or Imaginative

- Trusting or Suspicious

- Tough-minded or Tender-minded

plus 11 other factors.

Another questionnaire developed in the US is known as the 'Myers-Briggs Type Indicator' (MBTI). It was designed explicitly to make it possible to test C. J. Jung's (1921–71) theory of psychological types and put it to practical use.

Test Administration

The MBTI, 16 PF and FIRO-B have all been popular as have many other professional assessments. To administer and interpret these assessments, you must undertake training with a test publisher or distributor which is authorised to provide you with the test materials.

Since 1970, there has been increasing use of computers in designing, administering, scoring, analysing and interpreting questionnaires. Recent developments are the 'OTP' (Occupational Type Profile) developed by Selby Mill Smith, the 'OPQ' (Occupational Personality Questionnaire) from Saville and Holdsworth plus other specialist questionnaires which will measure whether an individual presents a security risk to an organisation or if they have particular tendencies towards being innovative and creative. There are now over 4,500 tests published.

The Increase in Popularity

Between 1984 and 1989 alone, there was a dramatic increase in the use of psychological questionnaires, biodata (biographical data) and assessment centre methods, such that there has been a threefold increase or more in the companies using these methods in at least half of their selection processes for managers. In this respect, the routine use of personality questionnaires by companies increased from 12% to 27% between 1984 and 1989. In 1996, the vast majority of listed companies use professional assessment techniques, instruments and methodologies.

Occupations and Psychology

Many years of research have tested various questionnaires which have been primarily aimed at the three areas of clinical psychology, educational psychology and occupational psychology. This report focuses on the latter, which is how people perform at work and methods by which to assess this performance.

To look at why 360 degree appraisals appear to be more than just fashionable in the UK and why the process is now being embedded into the culture of many organisations, we need to look back and see why we have arrived here. The reasons it is important to do this are as follows:

- As our thinking on staff development becomes more sophisticated there is a danger that we forget the foundations of that thinking and possibly view systems in isolation. To succeed in the future, you will need to be holistic.

- During the last decade, the UK has seen numerous new standards, ideas and initiatives which have attempted to revolutionise organisations. 'Initiative fatigue' has caused many people to be very sceptical of appraisals generally. To succeed in the future, you will need to overcome scepticism.

- No methodology including 360 degree appraisals can work without people having a good appreciation of what the system is trying to achieve. They also must support this goal. This means you will need to sell your concept well. To succeed in the future, organisations will need people to 'buy in' to the process.

Self-managed Learning

The reason you will need to understand the principals of performance appraisal and how it links to self-managed learning is that you may decide to link 360 degree appraisal to a person's pay packet. This naturally is a contentious area and unfortunately there are no golden rules. This means that your company's policy will be shaped and agreed by you and whoever else is involved in that process. For 'best practice' to prevail it may be wise to study as many cases as possible to form an individual opinion for what will work for you.

As you may already be aware, there have been various accepted models of performance appraisal used by companies both here and overseas to assess people at work. In a recent book published by the Institute of Personnel and Development (IPD), *The Performance Management Handbook*, you will find good examples of models and processes relating to this subject. Mairin Gannon in her chapter on personal development planning writes about the growing need for personal development:

> Increasingly, organisations are stressing the need for employees to take responsibility for planning their own personal development. There are numerous reasons for this growing interest in personal development. In organisations in which there is an emphasis on reducing headcount, it is critical that the remaining staff remain motivated and empowered to deliver stretching objectives.
>
> In organisations facing dramatic change, employees often have the best understanding of the development they need to deliver the organisation's objectives. In organisations that are de-layering, traditional career paths are perceived as ebbing away, and employees need a process that encourages them to think of new models of development to enhance their skills and ability to deliver to the organisation. Above all, many organisations are seeking to create a culture in which people have an interest in and ownership of their own learning and development.

1.2   The Organisation

Company Culture

Within most organisations, whether they are public or private sector, it is now widely recognised that a particular 'culture' exists. 'The way we do things around here' is a phrase not only used at IBM. 'Culture' in its organisational sense really refers to the collective behaviour of the people within that organisation and generally refers to the 'accepted behaviours' of those working together.

If, over a period of time, people have developed particular behaviours deemed to be appropriate for the organisation's success and the company still makes a profit, they are unlikely to consider that any change in their own behaviour is necessary. In fact, it is unlikely that people generally really volunteer to change their behaviour patterns. Perhaps the reason they joined that organisation is indeed because of its past success. These individuals may then naturally try to 'fit in' with their peers and superiors.

Within a unionised environment there will be agreed procedures to follow if members need to speak with management. With smaller firms, the managing director may work in the same office as other members of staff. In many firms, change seems to occur often yet within others infrequently. Frequency and type of change naturally play a part in how people are feeling and thinking at work and this is bound to have an effect on their general performance.

Your organisation's culture will play a large part in deciding how you implement 360 degree appraisals and it is strongly recommended that you look at the history of what has been introduced to staff already by way of assessment processes. Therefore a complete review of the systems and procedures that have already been in place along with opinions of how successful they have proved to be will be useful if only to make you aware of issues which may cause possible pitfalls and problems.

Company Structure

As companies have adapted to changing economic conditions, one particular change has been to introduce systems and processes which will enable people to be in control of areas of responsibility which were traditionally handled by their training or personnel department, for example staff selection and development. These two areas used to be handled by a central function in some companies and have now been 'devolved'. This means that line managers hold more responsibility and actually do more of their own hiring and firing.

In some companies this trend has reversed itself and the responsibility has shifted towards a central function again. In most multinationals, there has been a tendency to localise, internationalise or globalise, each method bringing its own complexities in terms of how people are recruited and then selected for promotion or training and development. In many instances, organic growth or a strategic merger has brought with it numerous problems and issues about how careers are managed internally.

Add to all this the concept of 'outsourcing' – the buying in of services traditionally associated with in-house departments – and you have a different world in business than that of only ten years ago. Flatter structures mean fewer people dealing with more complex projects across new and emerging social, political and business boundaries. Arie de Guess, former chief planner at Shell, has suggested that the key to business success is the ability to learn faster than competitors, and that the key to learning faster is to run plenty of 'experiments on the margins'.

The marketplace will always punish product failures. If, however, leaders punish individuals and work groups for trying something new, any spark of creativity or innovation is tempered. In contrast, creating a culture where people who take prudent risks and publicly share their learning from set-backs and then receive rewards and not retribution is a daunting and vital task for any executive.

Seizing Opportunities

Regardless of its strategic goals and noble intentions, there is literally no way for a company to seize opportunities if it is saddled with an overly layered, overly centralised and overly functionalist structure. An 'out of condition' person who reads every running book available and buys the ultimate in high-tech clothing, is still 'out of condition' at the starting line in the 100 metre dash.

Therefore, decentralisation versus centralisation, devolvement versus centralised ownership of staff development, and changes in economies will continue to impinge on how companies compete in the future. So to ease the process of introducing 360 degree appraisal well, you will need to engage in some form of 'culture mapping' process which will involve organisational development in its broadest context. This will assist you to think about how an organisation can be prepared to respond to commercial opportunities which may occur.

1.3   The Problem With a Good Idea

Initiative Fatigue, a Common Failure

This in some organisations will be your biggest problem. Here are just a few of the types of initiatives and buzzwords which have hit business in the last five years (some go back a little longer):

*   Total Quality Management

*   Kaisen

*   Visions and Values Exercises

*   BS 5750

*   ISO 9002

*   EN 27000

*   BS 7850

*   Business Process Re-engineering

*   Culture Change Programmes

*   Visionary Refocusing

*   The Learning Organisation.

Many of these programmes have looked at documentation systems and tried to find a way for companies to identify the best type of system for them to prove they have some form of quality standard. Some of these programmes have been used to change the way organisations are structured and with these changes look at new ways to improve how things are achieved. So, for example, supply chains may be reinvented, new task teams may emerge for specific projects, people may be on secondment to other organisations for a short period to develop a new skillset or some managers may embark on a full-time or part-time course of study such as the Masters in Business Administration (MBA).

Many of these processes have evolved around both individual and organisational development but, critically, most of them have been about general issues of organisation development rather than specific issues of people development, with the exception of the 'learning organisation'. Arguably, people have tried to be specific and link their own development plans to the business plan of the organisation, but personal development is a much wider issue than simply the organisation for whom the individual is working for today.

Lack of Commitment

One of the most common statements made by people who are not performing in an organisation is: 'I didn't fully understand what was expected of me'. Yet it may have been the case that the individual attended training programmes or meetings where full explanations and instructions were given. The reasons for this happening are explained in many ways, for example: was the individual listening properly? was it well explained? or was sufficient time allowed within the schedule to achieve what was expected? Loyalty and commitment occur for various reasons and one way to develop these values is to achieve a good contract from the beginning. One phrase often used by consultants is 'buy-in', which leads in turn to commitment.

The Contract

This may also be expressed in many different ways, for example: 'employment contract', or the agreement between people to carry out a task. One way to avoid failure with systems such as 360 degree appraisals is to ensure that people actually want to take part in the process. There has recently been new research about the concept of the 'psychological contract'. This is the type of contract which will be necessary for you to make with employees to assist you to manage expectations.

Selling 360 Degree Appraisal

If you do not feel confident to sell this concept with confidence, you must examine and question the reasons why and find a solution. The consequence of you not doing so will be failure. Selling concepts and theories is very much a part of human resource management or personnel and training and is a contentious area which brings into question professional ethics and standards. This questioning is positive when it occurs, as the raising of the question allows people to decide exactly where the organisation is in terms of its ethical standards.

Buy-in and Ownership

So, for any appraisal system to be successful you must achieve 'buy-in' and ensure that everyone involved in the process understands why they are taking part. The unique difficulty which 360 degree appraisal presents is that by definition it requires the buy-in and commitment of everyone in the organisation. Also how people will take part and what the benefits will be to themselves and the organisation must be clearly understood.

Please note it is also important for people to be allowed to question all of this and be given answers which they can understand and come to terms with. There have been initiatives costing thousands, tens of thousands and millions of pounds which have been specifically designed to train and develop people to make a company more successful than its competitors. Sadly, much of this money was either wasted or the outcomes or outputs of such initiatives were not closely evaluated and therefore it is difficult for anyone to prove whether the money was well spent.

Perhaps again the problems of 'ownership' have been the issue. So, again, looking at the structure, you need to ask yourself the question: 'Do the people in this business believe in and own the process or initiative going on here, or do they feel as if someone is really trying to get them to do "more for less" and contribute to shareholder value at the risk of their personal careers and health?'

Professor Norbert Walter is Chief Economist at Deutsche Bank and at a speech made in London in 1995 he predicted: 'Three career changes and eight job moves will be the norm in the future.' Most futurologists and thinkers, be they management gurus or otherwise, will have a view on where careers are going and, as Professor Walter suggests, the general accepted theory seems to be that change is here to stay for a while.

Change

As the trend in organisations has been to cut back rather than invest, organisations have embarked on numerous initiatives to increase productivity at little cost. Clearly it has not all been doom and gloom and we have seen investment in some areas both geographically and by industry sector, yet the trend has, without question, been for change.

This change has affected people and organisations more quickly than before and has left many with conflicting thoughts of change itself. So again a holistic approach is necessary if your appraisal system is to be successful and overcome any scepticism which may have already emerged as a result of bad experiences or unfair systems, in the past, which may have been developed and introduced into the company or the organisation new employees last worked with.

This challenge is certainly not to be underestimated or ignored. Even if you feel that buy-in has occurred at a sufficient level and depth by enough people, when it comes to implementation and thorough examination of the data, you may find that you have overestimated people's commitment to the plan. The scepticism which may prevail is understandable. Between 1990 and 1995 British industry embraced change in a way very different from before. It made swathes of 'middle management' redundant. Traditionally these were the people who kept organisations going in turbulent times and these were the individuals who used to make others redundant.

This change in fortunes for people from many different backgrounds has awakened, or some say enlightened, the UK to new global pressures which it had shielded itself from for many years. With the privatisation policies and other social changes, Britain is now transforming itself into the Hong Kong of Europe – a small island, attached to a large mainland by a tunnel, where people can be enterprising and 'make things happen' as individual entrepreneurs.

Human Motivation

There is a wealth of information written on human motivation. You need at least a basic understanding of this subject for you to be successful in implementing any appraisal system. This means not only in terms of how much you know, but also how you apply what you know. Theories from Abraham Maslow and Herzberg have been debated for years and there has been a general movement towards the 'value' based organisation.

If you take any market trader selling household goods and analyse what is actually going on in terms of staff selection and appraisal, it does not seem to be particularly removed from what happens in larger corporations. People are making judgements about others. The language used may be different, yet the values of the people working together seem to play a large part in the success of the company, especially if they are working in the same direction. The market trader will have their own method of assessing a worker's ability to sell and maintain a good range of products, and the chief executive of the oil company will assess her/his sales director based on a different set of criteria. One thing is for sure, neither can afford to get it wrong too often.

Power and Influence in Organisations

There are numerous writings on power and influence in organisations and this subject is useful to understand if only to appreciate some generalist theories on the subject. The reason this subject area could be of use is that you will need to understand, identify and anticipate levers for change at some stage when you introduce 360 degree appraisal.

A Hierarchy of Power and Influence

Take these four levels:

1.   Punishment and reward

2.   Assertive persuasion

3.   Trust and participation

4.   Common vision

Level one, punishment and reward, is a management technique which has been around since management itself. A typical example might be a subordinate refusing to do what she/he is asked. Some type of privilege is taken away or conversely if they 'do what they are told' they receive something to reinforce this type of behaviour. Most of you will have come across Professor Skinner and his famous experiments with rats which identified this as being 'classical conditioning'.

Level two, assertive persuasion, is where one individual manages to persuade another to do something by being assertive in their manner. Perhaps the individual who is being persuaded feels overawed, overpowered or under the influence of the individual and will readily respond to almost aggressive behaviour to 'keep the peace'.

Level three, trust and participation, occurs when the individuals themselves feel comfortable with participating together in whatever project and have developed sufficient trust in each other's opinions and actions that they willingly assist each other. They do not feel the need to constantly question each other's motives and believe that others respond in the same way.

Level four, common vision, is what many organisations try to achieve. It is where everyone understands the strategy, tactics and direction the company is taking and for what reasons. It assumes that people will understand exactly what is expected of them at all times and focuses everyone's mind on the predetermined goals. These goals are also known to all.

If you look at these four levels as within a hierarchy, you can see that level one is easy to achieve and in ascending order they become increasingly more difficult. The reality is that it is very difficult to move 'up' the spectrum to level four, but very easy to slip backwards to the previous level.

360 degree appraisals may work whichever stage your organisation is at. However, it will probably be much more likely to succeed if the environment is in either level three or four. It just seems to make the introduction, acceptance, performance and evaluation more real and understood. Therefore it is recommend that you get to grips with these issues before you even attempt to introduce an appraisal system which will undoubtedly rely on a great deal of trust between people.

Value and Dissatisfaction

Getting it wrong implies a value judgement on what is good or bad but in the context of people at work we are not making judgements about people's intrinsic worth or virtue. We mean the 'fit' between a person's goals and the values of an organisation.

Equality and Reward

Most managers realise it is virtually impossible to ensure all employees are equally rewarded and satisfied. One school of thought suggested by Nicholas Imparato and Oren Harari in their book *Jumping the Curve* is that not everyone should be equally rewarded and satisfied. 'The organising principle insists on nothing less than the strategic management of job satisfaction and dissatisfaction. For the individual manager, a key responsibility is thus quite literally to shape an environment where the "right" people (those committed to the desired culture and vision) are satisfied, successful and secure, and where the "wrong" people (wrong for your organisation – those who oppose the culture and vision) are not.'

Research shows that attempting to influence people only with pay, praise and promotion (carrots) or punishment (stick) is shortsighted. The mass of findings in organisational psychology is quite clear: motivation is primarily intrinsic. That is, individuals' motivation to work hard, feel conscientious and be creative on the job is primarily dependent on such factors as how challenging and interesting their work is, how much control and autonomy they have on the job, and how much opportunity they believe they have to learn and develop on the job.

So, to ensure there are a range of different employee experiences, companies must provide different opportunities for intrinsic rewards (growth and self-directed work) and extrinsic outcomes (pay, praise, constructive feedback and promotion). Here is a simple example of how this may work in an organisational context:

Manager A and Manager B Both Work for the Same Organisation

The criteria for success as a manager has been defined as:

1.   Initiative

2.   Teamwork

3.   Quality control

4.   Staff development

5.   Contribution to the bottom line

Both managers are assessed and the following ratings are given on a scale of 1-10:

Manager A	Manager B
7	5
6	3
8	5
9	2
6	3

In order that Manager A will feel and experience a sense of psychological 'fairness' or equity, she/he will need to feel more rewarded and appreciated than Manager B. (At this point do not forget that some people naturally require more recognition than others as the FIRO-B suggests.) It could be argued that if the company fails to discriminate between the performances of A and B, this not only diminishes Manager A but also reinforces what may be complacency in Manager B. Manager B's performance may turn out to be the lowest common denominator of performance standards.

Often, what has happened in organisations is that the best contributors have become cynical and frustrated about the organisation as they become more and more upset about the inequities. The consequence is that often superior performers and the most talented people are the greatest contributors to figures of high staff turnover.

If you think about the costs of hiring and training a replacement every time you lose a 'good one', this will normally run into tens or hundreds of thousands of pounds – costly in financial terms, in strategic terms and emotional terms. What the individual leaves behind is also important. In *Healing the Wounds* by Noel Bain, there is great mention of the 'Survivor Syndrome'. This is how the varying methods of redundancy packages have hit the employees left to carry on after their colleagues (and often friends) have left. This type of emotional pattern will also occur when a high performer goes.

Is This the Only Way to Succeed?

There is room on the planet for different organisations, formed for different reasons and managed in different ways. It may be that when you examine your own company, there are numerous sets of cultures which need nurturing in various ways. A 'Cabal' or 'culture within a culture' may be critical to the success of particular organisations and may not even be recognised by people within the company until after it has been 'outsourced'.

Also, 'survival of the fittest' cultures are not always the ones which are best. The theory is that people are out to satisfy their own egos rather than thinking of what is best for the company.

The Message of Consistency

People in organisations remember the following and they remember for a long time:

- Who was hired.

- Who was demoted.

- Who was confronted.

- Who was upset.

- Who was confused.

- Who tried their best.

- Who was applauded.

- Who was promoted.

- Who was fired.

They also remember who got the attention from management and who got the best assignment.

How This Relates to Performance Review

During appraisals, people may feel or experience a distinct lack of consistency about the process. Some reasons are that certain individuals will have a better rapport with their boss and others (who may be performing better) have poor boss handling skills. Certain senior managers may also devote much more time and possess a genuine intent to assist their subordinate's development. Hence, certain individuals may conclude the organisation has no priorities, or is unsure of its priorities, or displays hypocrisy. This will often mean the company will suffer in terms of organisational integrity, coherence and performance.

This is because people find the lack of consistency between stated purpose and actual practice truly debilitating. Researchers James Kouzes and Barry Posner note that the etymological root of the word credibility is credo, meaning 'I trust, I believe.' Their research leads them to conclude that 'credibility is mostly about consistency between words and deeds. People listen to the words and look at the deeds. Then they measure the congruence. A judgement of "credible" occurs when the two are constant.'

A Sense of Relief

There is often a great sense of relief, warmth and goodwill when a leader is willing to define purpose and act consistently. This not only applies to the managers, but also the top performers and employees at every level. This kind of unification of vision is an important element of the leadership mix and therefore, with 360 degree appraisals and their associated processes, the organisation will not only be talking good people development, they will also be walking it.

Feedback

If you ask people to provide feedback on another person's performance there are a number of reasons as to why they will find it difficult. One of the reasons is general embarrassment. Unless you have been used to the concept of 'feedback' in theory and practice, at first you may find it difficult to perform with any degree of usefulness. If people are not used to giving and receiving feedback, they may find this process very uncomfortable. This element of 360 degree appraisal is probably the most crucial to its success and you are therefore strongly advised to seek the assistance of a feedback specialist or book yourself onto a training programme soon.

Feedback is all about communicating to one individual how they are viewed by another. There are numerous models of feedback and they may be verbal, non-verbal, written, expressed or implied. As most of our communication is non-verbal and people 'see' or 'perceive the world' through their own set of filters, what you deduce from an individual's actions may be entirely different from someone else. This really is the essence of 360 degree appraisal as the idea is to create a consistent method to assess an individual's performance at work, using the collective judgement of people around the individual.

I do not wish to skip over 'feedback' as a subject, yet it is one of those where there really is no substitute for the real thing and as professionals you must ensure that people within your organisation are trained to give and receive feedback by qualified and experienced professionals, otherwise the benefits from any appraisal system will be questionable.

How Feedback May Work

The quality of feedback is just as important as whether the person receiving the feedback feels like listening or not. Whether or not the individual feels like listening will partly depend on whether or not they respect the opinion of the person providing the feedback or perhaps if they can link what is being said to their individual performance or personal competence. One question that may be raised is if an individual wishes to give or receive feedback, is it best that they control its flow? For example:

- Who gives feedback?

- When is it best given?

- Why is it given?

- How is it given?

The above will greatly depend on the maturity of the individual plus so many other factors, which leads me onto the next, but equally important, issue. The whole purpose of designing the system well is to make it work. Therefore, perhaps the most important issue needs to be – will people act upon the results?

One of the simplest and most basic methods of instruction on this subject is for people to understand the importance of providing a little good information, a little constructive advice followed by finishing with something positive. The first piece of this feedback will ensure that you have the individual's attention. The second is what you want to say which might give the individual some helpful thoughts about how to improve their performance and the last is designed to assure them your intentions were helpful and not to criticise for the sake of it (or any other political agenda you may harbour).

Assertiveness and Feedback

With some individuals it may be necessary to take a more assertive approach. This is a complex area and can lead to great frustration, misunderstanding and areas of personal discomfort. Indeed, asking people to 'step outside their comfort zone' is what many practitioners spend their time doing in order to assist behavioural change. This whole area is fraught with issues and problems which, I believe, are better handled with face-to-face instruction and the advice is, if you do not understand assertive feedback processes, get some good instruction.

Feedback in a Multi-cultural Environment

As we now move to multi-cultural organisations, you will also notice how multi-cultural sensitivity will be a critical factor to determine the appropriate style of feedback. For example, humour may be used very effectively during the process of feedback. Yet what is funny in some cultures is plain rude in others. Also, certain cultures feel that criticism of older people is unwise and disrespectful, yet others see it as healthy and part of growing up. Again, it is important not to judge whether or not one culture is right or wrong, as this will not easily fit organisations today, but to think through and look at acceptable norms and tolerances which people may have.

The sensitivity of some individuals and their reaction to feedback is of serious importance. Often people will not confess to being 'hurt or upset' in front of their colleagues and yet these are the moments which need the most sensitive handling if performance is to be maintained or increased. Recently, we have seen more and more evidence of what has been labelled the 'feminine' area of management practice. People today may or may not need assistance to develop personal qualities which may be perceived as traditionally 'belonging' to either gender.

There is evidence from psychologists which will clarify some small areas of differences between male and female managers, yet remember that areas such as sensitivity, tolerance and resilience are androgynous qualities or human weaknesses, depending on the moment and the reason. Perfect how your company deals with these emotions and issues and you will score over your competitors every time.

1.4   To Summarise

1.   Assessment is constantly evolving as a science.

2.   Professional assessment is learned and systematic.

3.   Professional qualifications are useful.

4.   Quality control of assessment is essential.

5.   A good test or measure will have data to support its validity.

6.   Do not assume all tests are reliable.

7.   Understanding performance appraisal is useful.

8.   You will need an appreciation of your company culture.

9.   You will need an appreciation of your company structure.

10.   There are predictable barriers to implementation.

11.   You will need an appreciation of human motivation techniques.

12.   Power and influence in organisations will be critical.

13.   Equality and reward policies will need to be addressed.

14.   Feedback techniques will need to be learned.

15.   You will need to think about people's sensitivity.

2 360 degree appraisal

2.1 What 360 Degree Appraisal Is and Comparisons With 90, 180, 270 and 450 Degree Processes

If you seek the advice of a consultant or expert, do not forget this methodology is only a few years old which means it is still establishing itself across a range of industries. Naturally one of the pitfalls you may encounter will be that a 'smart' consultant manages to sell you a 360 degree system which will solve every imaginable problem your organisation is ever likely to encounter in terms of people development. *Caveat emptor* – only through a fairly lengthy process of agreement between you, senior management, any union representatives, the entire personnel team, plus any consultants, facilitators, trainers or external providers of support can the introduction of 360 degree appraisal be a real success.

This also means the definitions below will be open to question until the methods and practices have been fully established and accepted by personnel generalists and specialists, whether they be theorists or practitioners.

A Few Definitions, Descriptions and Criticisms

90 Degree Appraisal

This is the traditional appraisal where an individual's performance will be assessed by their superior. 90 degree review has, in the past, been used by organisations to allow a structured meeting whereby the overall performance of an individual may be reviewed by her or his boss. Sometimes known as performance review or performance appraisal, personnel departments sometimes produce written guides or policy statements for line managers to use. Many personnel departments have 'devolved' this process to supervisors, team leaders or managers.

This 'devolvement' process is the pendulum referred to in organisations. Responsibility for staff development will switch from the personnel or training department to line mangers. You may notice the different policies and practices from organisation to organisation. This has occurred for many reasons but probably the most significant factor will be: 'If the senior management team can run the company effectively and profitably without a personnel or training department, they will.'

So whilst it has been the remit of training and personnel to foster and encourage line managers to appraise their own staff, this has not happened regularly, consistently and with sufficient skill for people to be developed to anywhere near their full potential.

The other reason that 90 degree appraisals do not always succeed is that 'follow-up' is a real issue. Corporations have been dealing with change which often has meant a reduction or freeze in recruitment. If productivity has been an issue, for example making more profit with less people, most members of staff will try to keep focused on their own tasks and not on developing others. In today's competitive environment, the attitude of many ambitious people will be to resist attempts to train or develop potential competitors. This has always been an issue with staff development and is probably one of the key problems any organisation faces.

180 Degree Appraisal

Also known as 'upward feedback', this concept has been around for a while. Basically, it is an opportunity for people to feedback to their superiors what they think of them. This process was used in a very unstructured form in the 1980s by British Rail and a number of well known UK corporations. At first it was acknowledged as being a quaint way to allow people to 'let off steam'. In reality, on many occasions it frustrated workers who wanted to provide constructive feedback to their superiors about customer complaints or real changes to be made, but found this 'one to one' process still tended to be 'boss and subordinate centred'.

If an individual is asked to comment on the performance of a superior who has the power to assist or destroy their career, naturally they will exercise some caution about what they say. If a high degree of respect and trust has been developed it will be easier for this type of appraisal to work. However, in some corporations, mutual respect, trust, co-operation and loyalty have been replaced by intimidation, harassment, political adroitness and cosy relationships, so this system of boss and subordinate relationship will work for some, but may tend to have a high degree of inconsistency throughout the organisation.

270 Degree Appraisal

This is new territory for many. This is where people seek and give opinions to subordinates and also peers. For example, a team of senior managers may appraise each other's performance and also that of their subordinates. Subordinates will also contribute to the process by commenting on the superior's performance.

Most of this type of feedback has, in the past, tended to be along the lines of 'I thought you did that particularly well, but have you thought about trying this?' All very well, but perhaps a little tame. There is nothing negative about the statement – in fact, it is classic or textbook feedback. But in reality it is someone making a suggestion. In today's business climate, it is everyone's job to make suggestions if they can add to the bottom line.

What 360 degree appraisal 'brings to the party' is something different than any other process and this can be explained in extremely simple terms, mainly because it is extremely simple. If you strip away the technology for a moment, we can look at the general theory.

360 Degree Appraisal

As the title suggests, 360 degree appraisal is a fairly rounded approach. It usually involves the individual, subordinates, peers and superiors. Most of the 360 degree instruments available will contain two key elements in the questionnaire. The first is a self-perception inventory and the second is how others see you. Clearly, it is the 'gap' in perception as to how others see you which will prove to be the contentious area and which may need careful handling. Notice I write 'may'. This is because some organisations will actually prefer the brutal approach.

> Managers, trainers, team-leaders, developers, or facilitators, can use 360 degree appraisal to make a contribution at a diagnostic level to assist to pinpoint particular areas of an individual's development. This means the analysis of training needs can be made with much more precision.

If people then decide to embrace the feedback given and act upon it, this may result in a noticeable change in behaviour. This is arguably the real and intrinsic worth of training.

450 Degree Appraisal

This is where the experts vary in their opinions. If you speak with a range of product and service suppliers, after questioning there is a level of inconsistency about the meaning of 450 degree appraisal. This is because as these processes evolve and become more established, 'branding' will become more secure. Generally speaking, 450 degree appraisal will include the following:

- self

- superiors

- peers

- subordinates

- customers

- suppliers.

What 360 Degree Appraisal Contributes

360 degree appraisal is able to contribute something which has never been available before in organisations. 360 degree appraisal is the systematic process of assisting personal development by the collective opinions of a range of people set alongside the opinion of the individual being assessed.

360 degree appraisal is potentially the most powerful self-development instrument ever used in the workplace. It also has the potential to be one of the most destructive instruments which could devastate an employee's confidence and self-esteem to a point where it could upset them psychologically. This means that you are advised to seek the assistance or advice of an experienced occupational or business psychologist.

Although the process of 360 degree review is entirely focused around one individual and how they may improve their personal performance, the 'added value' this may bring to the organisation is what many practitioners are interested in. So, for example, 360 degree appraisal may be used in the following ways:

- as a personal development instrument;

- as a staff appraisal system;

- as part of a culture change programme;

- as a way of unblocking poor communication channels;

- as a way to identify superior performance;

- as a method to introduce change;

- as a method to raise awareness of personal performance;

- as an instrument to predict job performance;

- as a way to assist an individual's career development.

Although this list is not a complete guide to the many uses of 360 degree appraisal it does show how versatile the methodology is. What the list does not provide for is how you use 360 degree appraisal in the context of the above. Here, it can only be pointed out that professional ethics will have a major influence on your choices. Let me give you an example, which is based on personal experience.

The managing director of a company asked me to produce reports on the performance of people who had attended a three-day training programme that I had designed and presented. I refused on the basis that delegates attending the programme were given to believe that anything they said or did during the programme was confidential.

Now let's examine my reasons. I ran the programme and built trust with the delegates such that they were willing to take part in an experiential learning exercise to develop their personal effectiveness.

All the delegates attending the programme were nervous because this was the first time any of them had undertaken an exercise of this type. It was apparent that they would perform better in front of their peers if they were relaxed and confident. This confidence was only to be achieved if delegates felt their own performance on the programme would not affect their future promotion within the organisation.

It was not for me to assume what delegates were thinking, yet as a professional I could see the fear and trepidation many of them were feeling about standing up in front of their colleagues and presenting in English (which was not their first language, in fact for many it was their third). Also, the personnel director mentioned that this was the first time any of them had experienced programmes of this nature. So in order to build trust and confidence, delegates needed to feel secure they could perform with confidence and the knowledge that neither the personnel director or the managing director would be able to judge them as individuals based on their attendance or performance on that particular programme.

When the programme was finished, I refused to produce the report based on the individuals' performance on the basis that, in my opinion, it would have been unfair to break the trust I had built between the training department and the delegates. I think at this point I became unpopular with the managing director yet my personal view still held.

This type of dilemma, especially with the confidentiality factor, is one which is bound to raise itself if you implement 360 degree appraisal. So, as professionals, you will need to clarify with your organisation exactly what your policy will be.

Organisational Policy and Confidentiality

This contentious area will naturally vary from company to company and if you look at the case studies you will glean from the way they have been written a little about the thinking which underpins the introduction of 360 degree appraisal. Policy review is a subject in itself and without setting out to provide comprehensive guidance on the subject I will refer you to check out what is policy at the Institute of Personnel and Development and leading complementary organisations in order for you to benchmark your own company against what is considered to be acceptable.

Your policy will partly depend on, but is certainly not limited to, the following:

- Whether you intend to be 'leading edge'. Will you be one of the first to implement 360 degree appraisal in your industry, or will you be following on after other firms have paved the way?

- What form of staff representation exists, for example works councils, industrial relations executives, unions, professional associations and informal representation?

- The current organisational climate. Has your firm recently made large numbers of people redundant or are you planning to do this? Will personnel see 360 degree appraisal as a way of identifying who to fire?

- Tactically and strategically, where are you at? For example, you may be planning a takeover, merger or acquisition, or perhaps you are being targeted. 360 degree appraisal may assist you to build confidence in certain areas of the company and provide people with deeper insight into how they will be seen by people from another organisation.

- Team building. Within organisations today, it is sometimes important to put together project teams quickly which can effectively deal with particular issues. 360 degree appraisal can allow people to 'get to know each other' much more effectively and quickly than other methods.

Professional Ethics - an Argument Against Appraisal

W.E. Deming is a well quoted academic and acknowledged expert in the field of Total Quality Management and in his book *Out of the Crisis*, published in 1986, Deming argues that performance appraisal can have a deleterious effect on employees:

> It [performance appraisal] nourishes short-term performance, annihilates long-term planning, builds fear, demolishes teamwork, nourishes rivalry and politics. It leaves people bitter, crushed, bruised, battered, desolate, despondent, dejected, feeling inferior, some even depressed, unfit for work for weeks after receipt of rating, unable to comprehend why they are inferior. It is unfair, as it ascribes to people in a group differences that may be caused totally by the system that they work in.

From the point of view of your organisational policy the subject of fairness and ethics will need to be discussed. It will be necessary for you to explore and discuss the reasons why, how and if you will introduce 360 degree appraisal with the most senior of personnel in order that a policy is agreed and communicated if necessary. This means the policy will have been negotiated and agreed before you try to pave the way for its introduction.

Policies are often ignored and sometimes not looked upon favourably by many people mainly due to the fact that an 'edict from above' takes away the very essence of an 'empowered organisation'. Perhaps no 'policy' but an understanding within the organisation that 360 degree appraisal will be voluntary at all levels with or without support from personnel professionals could be another way to smooth its introduction.

Standards

At present, no nationally recognised standards exist for the implementation of 360 degree appraisal; however, there are excellent guidelines on the subject of 'testing' set out by the British Psychological Society. These guidelines are mainly addressed at the introduction of personality measures or psychological questionnaires and clearly state what you must consider before using such instruments.

Competencies

The 'competency movement' started in the UK in the early 1980s as a result of numerous research projects carried out both here and overseas. Probably the most influential character is R.E. Boyatzis. Over ten years ago Boyatzis coined this definition, 'a competency is an underlying characteristic which differentiates superior performance from average or poor performance, a skill, trait, expression of knowledge or self-image'. From his landmark book published in 1982, *The Competent Manager*, many consultants, trainers and academics have wrestled and grappled with various theories and practices associated with competency in the workplace. There are numerous approaches to competencies and this has naturally led to some confusion. Within your own organisation, you will need to decide which particular approach will fit. Other definitions are as follows:

> An observable skill or ability to complete a managerial task successfully. (Jacobs)
>
> An underlying characteristic of a manager causally related to superior performance. (Evart).
>
> A superior level of managerial performance which is consistently displayed. (Klemp).

National Vocational Qualifications

In the UK we now have a system of work-based assessment which involves an 'assessor', a 'verifier' and of course the trainee. If deemed to be 'competent', the trainee may qualify for a National Vocational Qualification and various awarding bodies have agreed recognised standards by which people are assessed. Mainly, the assessments have been 'functionally' or 'technically based'. This means that an individual has proven to be 'competent' after the assessor and verifier have seen examples of the tasks performed by the trainee.

There have also been developments from the Management Charter Initiative (MCI) which incorporate 'behavioural competencies' into the equation. These standards provide some guidance as to how behaviour may be linked to good management practice. Note also that many firms develop their own competency frameworks to assist them to focus on what makes people successful (or successful people) within an organisational environment.

In November 1989, R. Hammond gave a presentation and defined competencies as 'not the tasks of the job, they are what enable people to do the tasks'. Hammond trained as a consultant with Hay McBer, a leading human resource consultancy practice and if, as he suggests, that 'competencies can be deep-seated qualities of people (motivation and personality traits)' this could be a sea change in the way we look at non-managerial roles. For example, many psychologists will accept the following theory:

From values people develop their attitudes and beliefs. From attitudes and beliefs, our behaviour patterns develop. To ask an individual to change their value set is complex and after an individual has reached maturity this is unusual. For example, if the individual has experienced significant trauma in their lives, such as bereavement of a loved one, or a personal attack, this individual may change themselves to adjust to the world around them. Please take note that the patterns of Post Traumatic Stress Disorder are now becoming recognised.

Therefore, for an individual to achieve a significant change in behaviour will probably mean a change in both attitudes and beliefs and also their values. This is likely to be a long term proposition and 'developmental' in training terms. These processes require complex modelling, planning and implementation and will probably not be achieved by a few courses alone.

Semantics and Confusion with Competencies

Many 360 degree appraisal products will be 'competency based' and this means that someone has decided which 'behaviourally anchored' competencies are best for people to be assessed against. Herein lies a potential problem. If, for example, you ask a range of people to assess an individual based on their personal perception against one of the above competencies, the question that you may have raised in your thinking is 'how do we know that one person's personal definition will be similar or the same as another's?'

Below are examples of three definitions of leadership:

- the ability to inspire others towards a goal;

- the ability to see the 'big picture' and translate that into easily understood objectives which people at all levels can comprehend, act upon and achieve their fullest potential under varying conditions to succeed with the task which they are given;

-            ruthless, domineering and tenacious behaviour which commands respect and on occasions fear, to ensure colleagues achieve what is necessary to compete and win.

Many definitions of leadership are possible. Margaret Thatcher defined leadership in 1995 as 'To serve and not to rule'. Different interpretations of these definitions are also relevant. For example, what is ruthless in one organisation is tame in another. What is inspirational to some may be boring to others.

Therefore, competencies which are 'behaviourally anchored' such as those defined by consultants in collaboration with organisations may produce different degrees of relative accuracy, depending on the internal understanding of what the words actually mean to the people using the system. This problem may be exaggerated when different languages are used in one organisation.

For example, the accuracy of the translation and the underlying meanings of individual words and phrases will be critical in terms of how people will be rated. What is competitive in the United States, France, China or India? Is 'good service orientation' the same in the UK as the US? Therefore, semantics and the precise definitions of particular words and phrases will vary depending upon who is asked.

Checks and Balances

If in one country an agreed competency may mean something very different than in another, this may lead to inaccurate or confusing feedback being given as one person may provide a rating of a person's behaviour based on what they thought the phrase to mean. One way to overcome this will be to introduce some form of 'balanced score-card' system. This will not be achieved without sufficient thought, preparation and planning and again it is recommended that you employ a consultant to assist if you have not undertaken this exercise before.

The relevance of this to 'best practice' is as follows. If you accept the theory espoused by Professor Warner Burke, which suggests that superior performance in an individual may occur when an individual's perception is concurrent with others in relation to their own performance, and if you also accept that semantics will also vary in how people are rated by others, then it could follow that:

-            It is necessary to conduct a detailed analysis of what people really mean by competence in the workplace. This will give people a framework of reference and a language by which to assess performance.

- Any attempt to change people's behaviour will be a long, arduous and potentially costly exercise and you may create a culture where people act as they feel they are supposed to act and not as they naturally behave. (The word 'naturally' is contentious in itself.)

- It could be useful to use rigorous selection methods to identify the underlying personality traits which an individual has and attempt to find 'optimal fit' which will result in less stress for the individual and better performance.

- With systematic planning, it may be possible to arrange for particular developmental programmes which will take into account where the business is going and which behaviours need to be encouraged and developed in individuals to assist this growth.

- Voluntary ownership of processes seems to achieve better commitment from people. When you are dealing with complex value sets and are asking people to visualise how an organisation relates to themselves and the world around them, it is not just ethical but also sensible to include their genuine conceptual thinking into the framework. Otherwise you run the very prevalent risk of turning 360 degree appraisal into another paper exercise which so many appraisal systems have become.

So, if your plan is to link specific competencies to 360 degree appraisal, you will need to build confidence within the organisation about how competencies actually work within the context of assessment. This will assist people to provide more reliable data for analysis.

2.2 Other Initiatives Which May Be Complementary to 360 Degree Appraisal

Other initiatives which will assist 360 degree appraisal to become embedded within your organisation are discussed below.

Investors In People (IIP)

This is an initiative promoted and sponsored by the Training and Enterprise Councils (TECs in England and LECs in Scotland) on behalf of the Department for Education and Employment (DfEE). Some professionals will argue that certain firms which have been 'leading edge' from a human resource development point of view have been 'Investing in People' for many years. Others will say it is a well packaged branding of 'best practice' for companies to follow.

IIP does have the added advantage of being partly sponsored by government and therefore the attraction of funding has encouraged many firms to adopt it. 360 degree appraisal is an excellent way to enhance self-development and will easily be introduced in the context of IIP.

Company Induction

If you are able, another way to start might be to ask people to complete some form of peer assessment soon after they join the organisation and ask them to do the same exercise either 12 or 18 months later. This could apply to newly appointed graduates, for example, and may provide assistance and feedback on a continuing basis to increase awareness of any areas of personal development.

Development and Assessment Centres

These have become more popular in the UK recently. There is a difference between an assessment centre and one which is purely developmental. Development centres tend not to be linked to any formal or informal assessment used to influence, decide or dictate a person's future career with the organisation; however, they are a way for the individual to identify and plan a strategy for their own development.

It has been suggested by one consultant who has been using 360 degree appraisal for over twenty years in the UK that 360 degree appraisal as a methodology was derived from the assessment centre processes developed by the armed forces in the 1930s in Britain.

An assessment centre may be used to decide which person to promote. For example, if there are 27 managers and three positions available at the next level which includes a higher salary along with a different set of responsibilities and skills, then some critical measures of personal performance may be appropriate. An assessment centre may typically include:

- in-tray exercises;

- psychometric assessment;

- problem-solving assessment;

- a team exercise;

- a group or individual presentation.

The data captured with 360 degree appraisal may also provide information to assist decision-making about whom to promote. Studies from Shackleton and Newell (1991) and Michael Smith (1988) clearly show that assessment centres will provide much better predictions about job performance than any other established methodology.

In 1988, Michael Smith conducted a study of studies (meta analysis) to take a critical look at selection methods in the UK. This study was designed to look at the predictive validity of selection techniques such as interviews, personality questionnaires and assessment centre methods. The table below shows his findings using the following rating scale:

0 = a fifty/fifty chance of prediction, for example flipping a coin.

1 = perfect prediction, for example every candidate chosen demonstrated 'optimal fit'.

Meta Analysis

Overall review of a large number of studies

0.65	Assessment centres (promotion)
0.54	Work sampling
0.53	Ability tests
0.43	Assessment centres (development)
0.39	Personality questionnaires
0.38	Biodata
0.23	References
0.19	Interviews

2.3   Various Methods of Implementation

When you research case studies relating to 360 degree appraisal, you are advised to speak with as many people as possible who have benefited from this methodology. If you are able to, it is recommended that you also speak with some individuals who felt it was not particularly useful. The reasons they give are probably the hurdles you will plan to overcome. Make no mistakes about what you are trying to achieve. You will attempt to implement a systematic process which will cause people to critically look at their own behaviours and listen and act upon the opinions of their colleagues.

Also you are asking people to spend time answering a series of questions which they may feel uncomfortable with. They will be asked to rate an individual's performance based on their personal experiences in dealing with that individual. They may or may not like the person they are appraising. They may see them as a threat to their own job security and may not wish to say or do anything which will show the person in a positive light.

If you do not prepare well, you will probably fail. How you choose to implement 360 degree appraisal, how you manage the feedback process and the reasons why you intend to implement such a system will affect the eventual outcomes. Here are just a few thoughts which you may wish to consider.

- What are your immediate objectives?

- What are your eventual objectives?

- Number of employees

- Industry type

- Age of company

- Age profile of company

- Education profile of company

- Company history

- The business plan

- Geographic profile

- Your budget

- Your timescale

- What you have been asked to achieve

- How you intend to integrate 360 degree appraisal

- What you intend to do with the information

- What you want to happen after you get the information

- The support you have from the top

- Will you link results to reward?

- Who will manage the process?

- What will your support mechanisms be?

It is critical that you build a system which will ensure that the feedback is managed in a balanced way. People from the organisation should be trained to give clear and balanced feedback which will assist and encourage personal development, rather than feedback which may erode personal confidence, competence and morale within the company.

The following two examples are at very different ends of the spectrum. It is recommended that you map a realistic picture of your organisation to focus your mind on its profile.

Company A

Reasons for implementation: Falling standards and profits.

Immediate objectives: To introduce 360 degree alongside current appraisal system

Eventual objectives: To replace the traditional appraisal system and to link competency reports to remuneration and reward.

Number of employees: 50   **Industry:** Financial services

Years trading: Five   **Employees' ages:** 16-42 (mean = 26.7)

Qualification profile: 38% graduates, 65% with a professional qualification.

Growth phase: New start-up

Target market: Young professionals

Budget to implement 360 degree appraisal: £150,000

Milestones and deadlines:

Phase one   - Months 1-3 - Conduct attitude survey.

Phase two   - Months 2-4 - Distribution and completion of 360 degree questionnaires.

Phase three - Month 5 - Collection and analysis of questionnaires.

Phase four   - Months 7, 8 and 9 - Feedback of results.

Phase five   - Months 8, 9 and 10 - Selected feedback from clients to the consultants about how well the process was managed.

Company B

Reasons for implementation: Steady growth in the UK with an overseas competitor seeking merger.

Immediate objectives: To increase sales by making the general sales team more aware of their strengths and shortcomings.

Eventual objectives: To add skills and knowledge to the general portfolio within the organisation such that any takeovers may be vigorously defended.

Number of employees: 50,000   **Industry:** Manufacturing

Years trading: 150   **Employees' ages:** 17-67 (mean = 42.3)

Qualification profile: 17% graduates, 32% with a professional qualification.

Growth phase: Product rejuvenation imminent

Target market: Large construction corporations

Budget to implement 360 degree appraisal: £500,000

Milestones and deadlines:

Phase one   - Month 1 - Source suppliers.

Phase two   - Months 1-3 - Identify planning team.

Phase three - Month 6 - Present proposition of 360 degree appraisal to the main board.

Phase four   - Month 7 - Identify team specialists within business units.

Phase five   - Months 6-9 - Write software program for local networks.

Phase six   - Months 6-9 - Train people in feedback techniques.

Phase seven - Ongoing - evaluate feedback standards.

Phase eight - Month 10 - Consultants run first feedback workshops.

Phase nine   - Months 11-15 - Company trained feedback specialists take over the process.

Attitude Surveys

The notion of putting together an attitude survey is not unusual prior to the implementation of any major change programme. Attitude surveys may be carried out by your own team or external consultants. The obvious pitfalls are whether the true attitudes of people are being surveyed, or the gloss which they believe you want to read. You will need to fundamentally examine how deeply you wish to explore employees' attitudes and for what purpose.

Most firms of occupational psychologists or your local business school may be able to provide you with a clear, concise picture of how your organisation looks in terms of the attitudes people have about a number of issues, from pay to promotion or management style. Attitude surveys may also assist you to prepare employees to consider the notion of being able to receive and give feedback as a way of improving work performance.

Phased Introduction

Other ways to introduce 360 degree appraisal include the introduction of 90 degree appraisal first, then 270. Time will always be an issue, as people will usually expect fast results, so how you chose to cascade or share information about 360 degree appraisal will certainly make a difference.

This is where you need to think clearly about two fundamental points: firstly the business plan and secondly the organisation development strategy. In many cases, these will be one and the same and in others there may be tactical and strategic issues which will impinge upon those plans. Examples are: Is there a board reshuffle planned? Are you in merger or acquisition mode? Are you about to demerger? Are there plans to headhunt new key personnel?

In a successful corporation today, it is common for at least one of the above to be in progress. You will really need to think, plan and schedule your implementation not only to fit around these changes, but also to take into account that people like to do a full day's work, have overseas assignments and sometimes take leave.

One way to overcome this is to start with the senior management team to build real commitment. The further down the organisation you go, you may find that people are less then co-operative about making this work. Think about how to overcome this. It might be that you will have certain 'leverage' points. These will be people who understand the need for staff development and find it useful from both an individual perspective and an organisational context.

The support you gain from such people needs to be fostered. However, the underlying danger is that some of these individuals may become more adept at abusing any system you create. The whole purpose of 360 degree appraisal is that collective subjectivity of an individual's performance will create objectivity.

Ways to Administer 360 Degree Appraisal

The way you choose to administer 360 degree appraisal is important for reasons of cost, control and confidentiality. Possibilities include the following:

- paper and pencil;

- screen administered;

- bureau service;

- external consultants;

- a mix of the above.

Choosing a Consultant

If your budget permits, you are advised to book a consultant for some advice. This is where you must exercise real caution for the following reasons. Any consultant worth their salt has studied hard to become a specialist in their discipline. One of the most common mistakes made by personnel departments is that they will call in a consultant, tell him or her they have a problem and expect the consultant to find the solution. The consultant puts a report together by which time the need has changed or the personnel department has learnt enough to 'have a go' themselves. The result is disappointment for the company and the consultant and an erosion of credibility for the personnel manager. The reasons are as follows.

The consultant will be experienced enough to put together a report which will highlight areas of need and will also provide recommendations. They are unlikely to provide you with genuine solutions unless you have contracted with them and paid an initial fee, or they have an ongoing commitment with your firm. Therefore, if you try to implement their suggestions and you are inexperienced, you will probably find yourself with more problems than you started with and will need to book more time with them to bail you out. This naturally will be more expensive.

The best way to avoid this happening will be to write to the consultants requesting specific information or assistance and ask for their fee structure and preferred method of doing business. Be clear and open with them and you will probably develop a good working relationship which will really save you money, time and trouble in the short, medium and long term. In fact, I believe you will find that 'contracting' which is the psychological and legal process which occurs at the time of appointment for a consultant is the most critical factor for success.

The Origins of Consultancy

The foundations of modern British management consultancy have two main strands: finance and people. The assessment of people in consultancy terms derives from people like Frederick W. Taylor (1856-1915) and Frank B. Gilbreth (1869-1924). It was these individuals which formed the basis for consultancy practices such as Inbucon in 1926, Urwick, Orr & Partners and P-E Consulting both formed in 1934 and PA Management Consultants which was formed in 1943. These four companies accounted for 75% of all consultancy work in 1956 when it was estimated that about £4 million annually was being spent on consultancy assignments and there were about 1,000 experienced consultants practising.

In 1982 the market had grown to £200 million annually with approximately 5,000 consultants. In 1996, most of the top 100 companies have used personality assessment, psychometrics or other methods of staff assessment with the consultancy industry now worth many billions (one estimate suggests the training industry alone accounts for £20 billion).

Back to Taylor. On his tomb at Germantown, near Philadelphia, the inscription reads 'The Father of Scientific Management'. Early in his life, Taylor's failing eyesight forced him to exchange an academic career for work in an engineering machine workshop. After serving an apprentiship, he was rapidly promoted until at the early age of 31 he was made chief engineer of the Midvale Steel works. There his curiousity was aroused about how people worked and he began to ask basic industrial questions such as, 'Which is the best way to do a job?' and 'What should consitute a day's work?'

One of the characteristics of a good management consultant is that s/he will question assumptions even if there is a risk of ridicule in doing so. Another is that s/he will apply logical processes to reaching answers no matter how trivial. Later, in 1898 Taylor went to the Bethlehem Steel Works and conducted an analysis of the 600 workers at the plant. He found, for instance that shovellers were lifting loads of 3.5 lb when handling certain types of coal but up to 38 lb when moving ore.

This drive for increased efficiency also inspired two other outstanding pioneers of scientific management, Frank B. Gilbreth and his wife Lillian. After Frank died in 1924, his wife Lillian carried on lecturing, advising and giving inspiration to generations of management consultants until her own death in 1972. Like Frederick Taylor, Frank Gilbreth was more than a mere theorist. He exchanged his studies at the Massachusetts Institute of Technology to become a junior apprentice on a building site. One of his early discoveries was the difference in methods used in laying bricks. He noted three distinct sets of movements were used by one craftsman:

- the first for slow working;

- the second for fast working;

- the third when demonstrating to a pupil.

He concluded that many of the movements were unnecessary and unplanned. He then conducted a systematic study to develop methods to reduce fatigue and increase output. During his first week at work, Gilbreth made so many suggestions about how bricks could be laid faster and better that the foreman repeatedly threatened to fire him. Gilbreth, however, persevered and within a year had designed a scaffold which made him the fastest bricklayer on the site.

What, you may ask is the relevance of this romantic story of a hundred years ago to 360 degree appraisals? When you think of 'time and motion' study the names of Taylor and Gilbreth will be in your mind and perhaps the next couple of paragraphs may assist your thoughts as you prepare for 360 degree appraisal.

One day, Gilbreth had a confrontation with Taylor's assistant. He discovered the assistant using a stop-watch to time bricklayers on one of his sites without asking permission. In Gilbreth's opinion, it was not entirely wrong to conduct a secret time study, but the assistant to Taylor had not even asked whether the study method was fully developed. The fact that records were being kept in Gilbreth's opinion was unprofessional as the methodology was yet to be proven. Later when Taylor suggested collaborating on a book, Gilbreth refused as he felt the differences in their styles and thinking were too fundamental to be resolved harmoniously.

Taylor then developed an interest in management problems after he realised the limitations of the worker restricted the potential productivity of the machine. Gilbreth, on the other hand, started with the human factor. His own concern for the human element was reinforced and supported by his wife's inclination and training. The husband and wife partnership discovered fairly early in their partnership that the best way to get co-operation from employees in a factory was to form a joint employer–employee board, which would make work assignments on a basis of personal choice and aptitude. It was also Gilbreth's suggestion that their marriage was to involve partnership in his work as well as partnership in the home.

What This Means Today

So, leap ahead again and substitute Taylorism for 'job evaluation' and Gilbreth for 'behaviourally anchored competencies'. The experiences of Taylor and Gilbreth are to illustrate a very simple message which is not supposed to get you 'fired up' or put you off implementing 360 degree appraisal. Its purpose is to reinforce both caution and care.

The parallel to be drawn is as follows. If a hundred years ago the pioneers of management consultancy were creating difficulty amongst their co-workers and, on occasions, being controversial, then understand that 360 degree appraisal and its associated concepts are relatively new in the UK and although specialists have created instruments which have been professionally validated, you will be the pioneer using them. If you are not an agent of change, find someone who is.

If, on the other hand, you decide to develop the instruments in-house, you will probably find that choosing a helpful and knowledgeable consultant will assist you to save time and money, providing that the consultant is frequently delivering this type of service and, the consultant understands that you want to keep ownership of the process.

Voluntary or Compulsory

It is useful to make clear the difference between performance and development. This will be useful to assist you to decide whether or not you believe a 360 degree process will be voluntary or compulsory. If you link your system to performance appraisal or developmental needs, the implications may be deeper than first imagined.

Performance management is an attempt to manage the needs of both the individual and the organisation. It is an approach to managing people using pay and performance within an agreed framework of:

- planned goals;

- objectives;

- standards.

This usually also means there is measurement, feedback and motivation. The issue surrounding 360 degree appraisal is that to link this system to performance and pay may lead to difficulty if imposed as a dictum or a 'must do' from management. Experience seems to show that some people will resist such methods as they may be seen as being divisive in nature.

The other and more favoured approach is linking your system to development. This word (development) seems to be used by management trainers and specialists quite often and for the purposes of this report I will define it as 'the process which adds knowledge or skills to an individual and changes they way they think and act to make them more employable or economically competitive or able to make a greater contribution to society than before.' This as you can imagine is a very personal issue and by definition the 'ownership' of this process rests with the individual or arguably the company which pays for this individual's development.

A Question of Ethics

This important question of ethics will arise if your organisation examines its policy thoroughly. You will need at some stage to ask the question, 'who owns the development process?' The significance of this question is important from the point of view of the 'psychological contract' which will occur, whether it is planned or not.

Taking into account professional ethics, practicability and a need to implement 360 degree appraisal, the task will be complex by definition. Firstly, you will need to obtain genuine commitment. Secondly, you need to keep 360 degree appraisal voluntary if possible. Thirdly, you must decide whether to keep it separate from performance reviews, remuneration and reward, promotion prospects or any tangible benefits in order to keep the process pure. This now represents a challenge which is theoretically easy to write about, but extremely difficult to implement. I hope you will read from the experiences of others that it is actually possible to achieve with patience, persistence and proper planning.

2.4   To Summarise

1.   360 degree appraisal is the systematic collection, analysis and interpretation of feedback on an individual's performance from a range of sources.

2.   It is a powerful self-development instrument.

3.   It may be used in a variety of ways including to assess superior performance.

4.   Confidentiality may be an issue with 360 degree appraisal.

5.   Professional ethics will dictate company policy.

6.   Competencies are a way to give people a framework of reference by which to identify performance.

7.   National Vocational Qualifications are competency-based accredited programmes which provide a simple model to follow.

8.   Some competencies are 'behaviourally anchored' and confusion could arise from the semantics of the language used.

9.   Checks and balances in your approach will assist to provide balanced and useful feedback.

10.   Voluntary ownership of the process seems to produce higher levels of commitment to the process.

11.   360 degree appraisal may be used at induction, assessment or development centres or as part of an annual appraisal plan.

12.   A meta analysis clearly shows that interviews are a low predictor of job performance.

13.   Thorough research needs to be conducted before the implementation of 360 degree appraisal.

14.   Consultants are useful provided that you choose with care and manage the relationship.

15.   360 degree appraisal may be linked or embedded into various initiatives including performance management and Investors in People, or used as a lever for change.

3 Products and services

3.1 Products and Services Available

These may be purchased from the UK or overseas. Broadly they will fall into two areas:

- test publishers and suppliers;

- trainers and consultants.

The test publisher may also be the supplier, or they may have authorised or trained others to use their systems. This may be under licence and part of the fees you pay will probably ultimately go the the test publishers. The research and development costs of good instruments are high (conversely, in poor instruments low) and naturally the authors and researchers need to recoup their costs.

Trainers and consultants may be generalists or specialists. Currently the marketplace has a number of specialists which deal in 360 degree products and some of these specialists designed and developed the products themselves. Others did not. For quality control, you must identify different parts of the process and assess your suppliers on their skill/knowledge set.

This will partly depend on the following:

- the number of years experience the consultant has;

- the qualifications they hold;

- the amount of focus their business gives to 360 degree appraisal;

- the amount of experience they have in your industry sector;

- what past clients say about them.

To a consultant, each client will be different and their needs will not be met in the same way with the same methods. There are some basic guidelines for consultants to follow, but if the client has complex issues to resolve, the consultant may try a new technique. If you assist with this flexible approach, you will probably also acquire skills and knowledge and you may encourage the consultant to transfer competency to you. Also, you may wish to assist the consultant to conduct critical research which will assist their own product development. This collaborative style of working is a good way to keep costs to a minimum and trust to a maximum. The business relationship with any consultant is to be valued.

Here is a simple checklist for consultant selection:

- a working knowledge of 360 degree appraisal;

- good communication skills;

- high expertise in facilitation;

- an ability to present their ideas, concepts and theories in a succinct manner;

- able to keep sensitive information in confidence;

- flexible and responsive to your needs;

- not overcommitted, that is not too busy to provide good service;

- someone who you can trust and confide in.

The reputation attached to your consultant is also a complex issue. For example, many consultants who do their work well sometimes become unpopular. This may be because they are willing to say things which people do not want to hear. Clearly, some individuals may find a particular consultant's tone, manner and delivery uncomfortable. This means that you need to be clear in your personal opinion that you are able to work with the consultant or the company they represent.

Broadly, products, services and sources of information fall into the categories listed below:

- questionnaires, both paper and pencil or computer-aided;

- bureau services;

- consultants such as feedback specialists;

- occupational psychologists;

- business schools.

Let's take a brief look at them one by one.

Questionnaires

These can be written by anyone. There are professional writers who specialise and have academic credentials plus research data to support the validity and reliability of findings and there are also people who will 'have a go' at putting a list of questions together. You can hazard a guess at which is the cheaper option.

There is a serious issue about cost. For example, it is not good practice to use any instrument which does not have the statistical reliability and validity information freely available. Yet, for some exercises, you may wish to 'raise awareness'. This may mean a short questionnaire to introduce the concept and allow your population to get used to the idea. If you do this, you are unlikely to derive any real value from the questionnaire although people may think they have (commonly known as the placebo effect).

The reliability and validity statistics will assist in proving that a professionally trained test author has written the questionnaire. These statistics may be used to correlate between instruments. If you are unsure about the validity of a particular questionnaire, ask to see the test validity research that accompanies the questionnaire. With some questionnaires there is also test and re-test validity data. If the company is not willing to provide you with at least a summary of that data, then seek advice from the Institute of Personnel and Development or the British Psychological Society.

With computer-aided assessments, ensure that you check all disks are virus free and that your company complies with the Data Protection Act.

Bureau Services

These are services offered by many of the test publishers. The publishers sell you the questionnaires and train you to administer them. You then send the questionnaires back to the publishers for analysis. The publishers then provide you with a detailed report based on the raw data supplied.

Consultants Such as Feedback Specialists

Firstly, qualifications in the UK are very confusing at the moment. For example, anyone can set themselves up as a psychotherapist with no qualifications, so who is checking up on quality?

Secondly, with evaluation in mind, how are you able to monitor whether the process managed by the facilitator really did make a contribution to the bottom line? Some consultants will also sell you concepts relating to 'linking human resource initiatives to the bottom line'. There are well documented cases yet few people are really convinced and will talk in terms of financial modelling and the assessment of people. 360 degree appraisal will achieve this and embed itself as a proven methodology in financial terms as soon as enough data becomes available.

Occupational Psychologists

These come in various shapes and sizes. A full description is available from the British Psychological Society. Generally speaking, psychologists fall into three main categories: educational, clinical, occupational. Other categories include: forensic and social. It now takes around eight years to qualify for chartered status, the longest of any profession in the UK.

The problem is that assessment of the 'expertise' or knowledge of a psychologist traditionally has been carried out by reading academic papers and assessing their reputation in the eyes of their peers and customers. Problems have occurred when the level of consultant has been too high or too low for the project and additional assistance has been added to the picture. This means additional costs. The safest way around this is to pay the consultant a fee to produce a full proposal and use this as part of your contract. Alternatively, you may wish to book the consultant on a retained basis.

Some consultants have been trained by psychologists to use instruments which have been specifically designed for one company. These 'bespoke' instruments may then be used for general use. If this happens, you must check the reliability data. For example, was the database of people for the study representative of the population you wish to assess?

Business Schools

A much underused resource, business schools are able to advise and assist with a number of human resource development initiatives. They understand how to attract government funding if applicable for your project and are able to bring information technology plus data handling capability to the team. Traditional business schools are becoming more commercial in their thinking and often have a range of consultants which they call on to assist.

Some schools are naturally more developed in their thinking than others so you will be well advised to treat them as you would a firm of professional consultants. As many professional consultants are also guest lecturers at business schools, the lines are increasingly blurred as knowledge and innovation spread from academics to business. On occasions they collaborate, and often they compete.

3.2   Choosing the Method for You

This is not actually possible to write about in a way which will benefit you or your organisation. The reason is simple. 360 degree appraisal is a process like numerous others and may be implemented in various ways for different reasons. Only by thorough examination of the issues raised in this report will you be able to make a reasoned judgement of what will actually work in your organisation. These are human issues and can only be understood with due consideration, time and a good level of professional assistance.

4 Case studies

4.1 Assistance with this Report

During the research phase of this report, I interviewed a number of people about their thoughts, feelings and experiences with appraisal and review processes. The participants were:

- personnel managers

- training managers

- human resource consultants

- company directors

- managers

- staff

- suppliers

- customers

- psychologists

- professional institutes

- universities.

During the period of research between 1994 and 1996, it was apparent that 360 degree appraisal had achieved numerous successes and also failures. The failures were for many reasons explained by:

- lack of resources;

- untrained practitioners;

- an underestimation from senior management about the time involved;

- an unwillingness to adapt processes to meet the changing needs of the business;

- not sufficient gravitas applied to the initiative.

4.2   Time Saves Money

It was found, however, that if planned and introduced with sensitivity, 360 degree review did make a positive contribution to people and organisations that was possible to evaluate in the short, medium and long term.

Most of those questioned found the voluntary approach easy to adopt and also felt that piloting 360 degree appraisal in a few different areas of the company useful. There was a tendency to prefer outside consultants to assist with the feedback processes although, as the range of people within the organisation became more skilled and knowledgeable about 360 degree appraisal, confidence grew.

One significant factor was related to performance. When people discovered that their own performance levels increased as a result of 360 degree appraisal, this increased confidence in the process. On occasions, those who did not benefit became isolated and some reported a feeling of alienation.

The 'face validity' appeared to be significant. (Face validity is when a questionnaire appears to measure what the questions are relevant to, for example, a sales assessment may ask questions relating to the individual's ability to persuade other people or if they enjoy socialising.) Also the balanced nature of the feedback and the variety of the assessors or respondents made a difference to the results. The type of rating scale was significant in terms of ease of use as was the style of administration. Most respondents to questionnaires felt that confidentiality was an issue, but this varied from company to company.

In a small minority of cases where extremely negative feedback was given about an individual, specialist assistance was used.

4.3   Industries Using 360 Degree Appraisal

During the project a number of companies were about to or had implemented 360 degree appraisal. These companies were in the following industrial categories:

- broadcasting

- financial

- entertainment

- automotive

- telecommunications

- consumer goods

- petrochemical

- defence

- health.

4.4   Examples of Best Practice

- Pages 56–9. Keith Bedingham, Director at Verax Limited, provided this case study featuring the Royal Air Force and the automotive industry. The case provides a good example of a 'high/low' study.

- Pages 60–5. Valerie Hammond, European Director of Human Resources at Johnson & Johnson, provided this example. Listed are examples of management success factors plus three pages from the questionnaire which was designed in-house.

- Pages 66–70. Peter Ward, Partner at Ward Dutton Partnership, provided this example. It is a couple of pages from an Individual Development Survey - II. Reproduced with courtesy from CCI Assessment Corporation.

- Pages 71–3. Adrian Atkinson at Human Factors International provided this example. It is two example pages from a computer report from a Professional Management Style Questionnaire.

- Pages 74–9. Andy Gillham, Human Resources Manager, Training and Development, at Mercury Communications provided this example. It is from the questionnaire which employees access via a network of servers and was designed in-house.

- Pages 80–3. Angela Brown, Director of Kerr Brown PDI, provided this example. These pages are examples from the 'Profilor' self-assessment questionnaire.

- Pages 84–6. Allan H. Church PhD, of Warner Burke Associates, provided this example. It examines the agreement or congruence between an individual manager's self-ratings on an assessment instrument and those obtained from a variety of sources.

Case Study

VERAX LTD

360° Feedback come to the Military

The origins of 360° feedback may lie in the Army's assessment centres, started before the second world war, but today's technology is being used to provide 360° feedback to some 6,000 RAF flying crew and 600 Army pilots.

Verax Ltd., working in conjunction with the RAF, have designed the Royal Air Force Behavioural Indicator. This gives feedback through a personalised computer processed report to both cockpit and ground crews. The feedback topics are CRM (Crew Resource Management) skills researched by the RAF as effective or counterproductive.

CRM skills fall into 3 categories - communications, team focus and decision making. Applicable to multi-crewed aircraft, between pilots in the same squadron and between ground and air crew, CRM skills have a significant role to play in improving safety in the air.

We believe that this is the first full-scale, systematic attempt by any military air force and army to provide CRM training and to build in a 360° feedback tool to that training programme. Re-measures may be used to quantify the amount of skill improvement which takes place.

360° Feedback helps improve car sales

Enclosed is a short case study using Life Styles Sales Force. This is a 360° feedback tool for sales people. The respondents can include customers, work colleagues, sales managers etc.

The important thing about this case study is that it shows a clear relationship between sales performance and certain dimensions measured by the 360° instrument. Apart from our own instruments, we are not aware of other instrument publishers showing relationships between their instruments and performance.

A CASE STUDY

In a recent study of luxury vehicle dealer sales people, it was shown that sales success appears to be related to their thinking styles. Results from self- and other perception questionnaires (an early version of the Sales Force Inventory) show that the more successful sales people are seen as humanistic and helpful, achievement-oriented, conventional only in certain ways and driven by needs for closure and a reasonable amount of perfectionism. In contrast, less successful sales people were measured as dependent on others, affiliative and socially-oriented (passive defensive).

As can be seen from Figure 1, respondents with high sales orientations (primarily the constructive styles) sold on average many more units than those with low sales orientations (primarily defensive styles.)

This study provided good preliminary evidence that the performance of sales people is related to the way they think about the world and behave. However, beyond the effects of thinking and behavioural styles, the performance of sales people also appears to be related to the characteristics of the organisation they work for. To some extent related to whether the organisations were well managed and effective organisations (see Human Synergistics-Verax Organisation Culture Inventory for further information), there appeared to be a relationship between the number of vehicles sold overall and the rating of sales training. Where rated "excellent" sales performance was higher than in those rated only "good" or "average". Although sales people from the same dealerships attended the same training programmes, they rated them differently. More units were sold in those organisations where sales people and managers saw their roles as clearly defined, where they reported a high level of participation in decision making and where pay and promotions were directly related to their performance.

360° Feedback helps improve car sales

A CASE
STUDY

Figure 1
Performance of People
with High vs. Low Sales
Orientations *

Number of
Units Sold
(2 months)

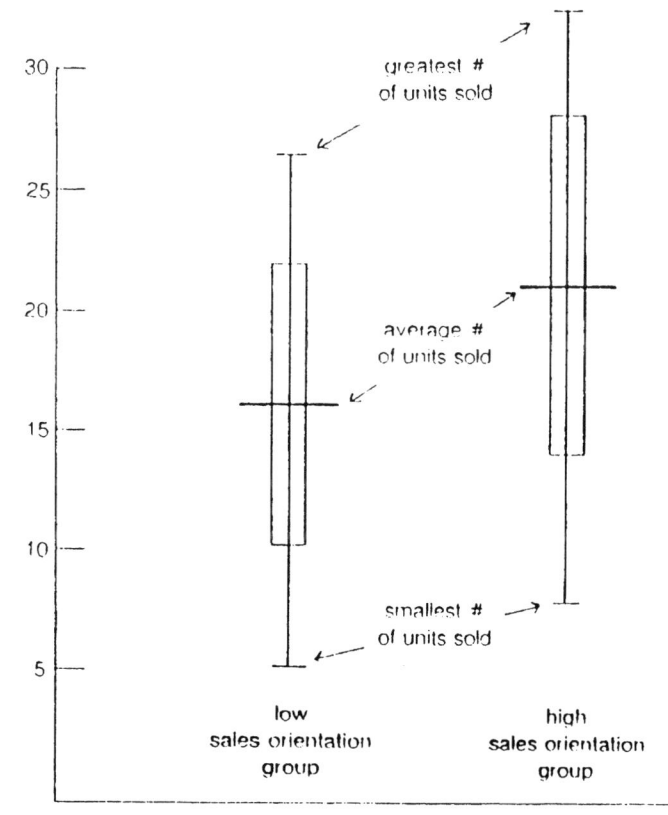

* *Sales people were broken into two groups based on their response to a*
  questionnaire measuring their "sales orientation". The two Continental
  *symbols above show the **greatest** and **smallest** sold by any individual within*
  *each of these groups. Also shown is the **average** number of units sold by*
  members of each of those two groups.

Case Study

JOHNSON & JOHNSON

JOHNSON & JOHNSON

DEVELOPMENT QUESTIONNAIRE

PRIVATE & CONFIDENTIAL

NAME OF INDIVIDUAL BEING ASSESSED

....

YOUR RELATIONSHIP TO HIM/HER

☐   BOSS

☐   SELF

☐   SUBORDINATE

☐   PEER/COLLEAGUE

☐   CUSTOMER

DATE OF COMPLETION: ....

This questionnaire is based on the Johnson & Johnson success factors. Please complete it for the individual concerned. Be as honest as possible. The information from this questionnaire will be used to identify individual strengths and development areas. Your answers will be treated with the strictest confidence and will not be directly fed back to the individual concerned.

Please answer all the questions; only leave a blank if you do not have sufficient knowledge to comment.

SECTION 1

Using the scale below please indicate how the individual being assessed behaves for each of the statements.

5.   Always happens
4.   Happens most of the time
3.   Sometimes happens
2.   Rarely happens
1.   Never happens
N/A   Does not apply or insufficient knowledge to assess

1. [ ] Sets challenging objectives which exceed previous standards

2. [ ] Anticipates problems and makes plans to avoid them

3. [ ] Identifies priorities and concentrates effort on them

4. [ ] Amends plans and work practices to accommodate new initiatives

5. [ ] Remains effective despite pressure of situation or workload

6. [ ] Champions ideas which will get breakthrough results

7. [ ] Consistently adheres to high professional standards/values

8. [ ] Provides constructive feedback to team members on how they are performing

9. [ ] Works well with other departments to achieve common goals

10. [ ] Makes good use of data to identify potential solutions to problems

11. [ ] Considers the risks and potential before making a decision

12. [ ] Develops ideas and strategies which improve customer satisfaction

13. [ ] Speaks up on issues of importance

58. ☐   Through actions, demonstrates commitment to the Credo

59. ☐   Does not give up until problems are solved

60. ☐   Has the resilience to see things through despite pressure of situation

61. ☐   Develops creative ways to improve using technology

62. ☐   Stands ground against opposition on importance issues

63. ☐   Gives clear instructions on what needs to be done

64. ☐   Successfully adapts to changing work environment or culture

65. ☐   Presents a tough message succinctly and with authority

66. ☐   Ensures that development plans are implemented

67. ☐   Gets team members to work together towards groups goals

68. ☐   Ensures that decisions are within our Corporate responsibility

69. ☐   Thinks in terms of customers' needs and the marketplace

70. ☐   Initiates change which is focused on business/customer needs

Johnson & Johnson

MANAGEMENT SUCCESS FACTORS

Leadership

- Communicates a customer - focused vision to others
- Shows a strong belief in own ability; works with little supervision
- Champions ideas which will get breakthrough results
- Inspires and motivates through setting a high personal example

Employee Development

- Ensures that development plans are implemented
- Coaches team members to improve contribution
- Gives feedback to team members on how they are performing
- Gives recognition for good performance or valuable contribution

Managing /Influencing Change

- Progresses beneficial change despite problems or setbacks
- Uses facts and rational arguments to influence and persuade
- Amends plans and work practices to accommodate new initiatives
- Successfully adapts to new working environment or culture
- Is an influential agent for beneficial change

Team Building

- Gets team members to work together towards group goals
- Selects team members with the right skills and ability
- Co-operates with other functions to achieve common goals
- Makes a significant contribution to team performance

Strategic Thinking

- Analyses business opportunities and develops sound strategies
- Thinks in terms of our customers' needs and the marketplace
- Updates strategies to reflect changing market/customer needs
- Uses broad knowledge of the business to make sound decisions

Planning/ Organising

- Plans for problems which might occur
- Puts resource in place to meet targets and sets deadlines
- Takes impact on other departments/operations into account
- Keeps measures of performance against targets

Integrity/Values

- Consistently adheres to a high set of professional values/standards
- Consistent in words and deeds :Follows through on commitments
- Takes responsibility for own decisions and mistakes
- Through actions, demonstrates commitment to the Credo

Johnson & Johnson

Delegation

- Identifies the priorities and focuses effort on them
- Provides clear instructions on what needs to be done
- Ensures work is achieved to a high standard
- Trusts others to get on with the task

Problem Solving /Analysis

- Uses information to quickly grasp complex problems
- Makes good use of data to identify potential solutions to problems
- Initiates action aimed at resolving problems
- Does not give up until problems are solved

Innovation

- Seeks improvements even in areas where results are good
- Develops creative ways of improving using technology
- Self starter - Sees to it that ideas are implemented
- Initiates change which is focused on business/customer needs

Judgement

- Considers the risks and potential before taking a decision
- Ensures that decisions are within our Corporate responsibilities
- Able to make tough decisions when required
- Makes good decisions even with limited data

Risk - Taking/Assertiveness

- Takes considered risks to achieve objectives
- Encourages risk-taking, does not penalise for genuine mistakes
- Experiments with alternative approaches and methods
- Speaks up on issues of importance; stands ground against opposition

Resilience

- Maintains effectiveness despite pressure of situation or workload
- Handles crisis situations constructively and efficiently
- Quickly bounces back from setbacks

Achievement Orientation

- Always sets challenging objectives which exceed previous results
- Pursues goals aggressively until they are achieved
- Sets and achieves high quality standards

Case Study

WARD DUTTON PARTNERSHIP

Organization Name _____

Individual Development Survey - II

Designed for individual contributors in such areas as: Engineering, Research & Development, Training, Marketing, Information Systems, Financial Services, Administration, Support, and Customer Service.

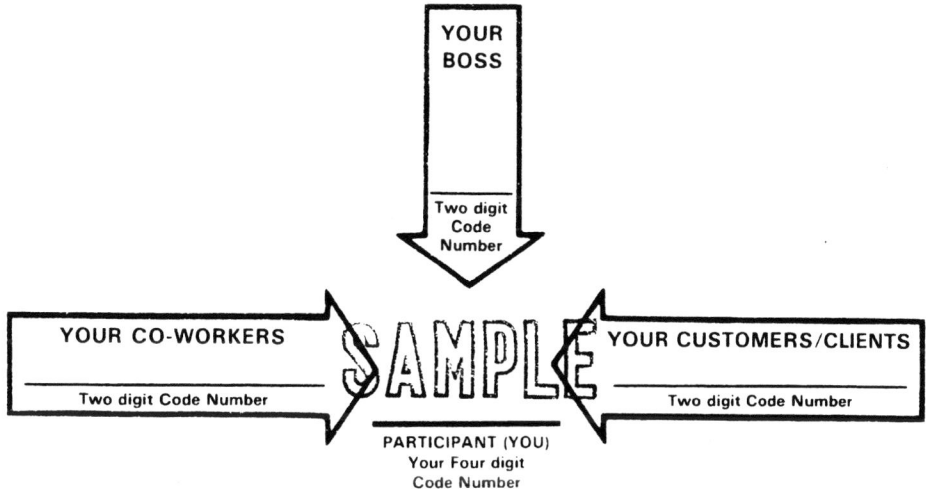

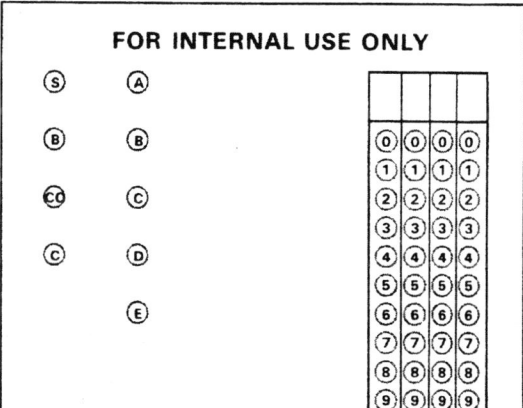

This survey is designed as a career and professional development tool. The feedback that participants receive will help them develop in their jobs. It is essential that your responses be as honest and candid as possible. Do not discuss your responses with anyone else.

> Please complete this profile within 48 hours and return it in the envelope you were provided. Thank you for your cooperation.

Instructions

There are two sections to the Individual Development Survey - II:

| A. IMPORTANCE RATINGS | B. PROFESSIONAL SKILLS AND PRACTICES |

- This section requests that you indicate the relative importance of eleven (11) critical skills *as you work with the person who asked you to complete this profile.*

- This section requests that you assess 60 key *behaviors you have observed in the person who asked you to complete this profile.*

NOTE: **Unless you are the "boss" of the person who sent you this survey**, your responses to both sections of this survey will be kept strictly confidential. Therefore, **you will not, under any circumstances, be identified to the person who sent you this survey.**

- Also, this is not a test. There are no right or wrong answers.
- Please complete and return this profile as soon as possible.

Directions: Your survey will be scored by an optical scanner. It is important you follow these marking directions.

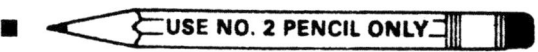

- USE NO. 2 PENCIL ONLY

- Do **NOT** use ink or ball point pen.

- Make heavy black marks that completely fill the circle. ●

- Erase completely any marks you wish to change.

- Make no stray marks in this booklet.

- Examples:

        Correct   Incorrect
    ①②③●⑤   ⌀⌀⌀⌀⌀

PLEASE DO NOT
WRITE IN
THIS SPACE

Part A. Importance Ratings

■ As you think about the person who sent you this survey, ask yourself, "**which skills are more important for this person to have when the two of you work together?**

■ Please try to distinguish the **more important** skills from those of lesser importance. *Try to use each of the five (5) columns as you rate the importance of each skill.*

> **Note:** if you are the person who sent these surveys to others, indicate how important it is for **you** to have each of these skills for your career or professional development.

Indicate how important it is for the person who sent you this survey to have each of the following skills *when the two of you work together*...

Extremely important
Very important
Important
Somewhat important
Not important

1. INITIATIVE AND RISK TAKING: The ability to demonstrate individual drive and accept responsibility for his or her actions . . . . ① ② ③ ④ ⑤

2. PERSONAL INTEGRITY: The ability to gain the trust and confidence of others by interacting in a fair and honest manner . . . . ① ② ③ ④ ⑤

3. QUALITY OF RESULTS: The commitment to produce high quality work (research, procedures, services, products) consistently, over time . . . . ① ② ③ ④ ⑤

4. PLANNING AND EXECUTION: The ability to organize and complete work within time and budget constraints . . . . ① ② ③ ④ ⑤

5. PROBLEM SOLVING AND DECISION MAKING: The ability to analyze a situation, identify alternative solutions, and make appropriate decisions . . . . ① ② ③ ④ ⑤

6. CREATIVITY AND INNOVATION: The ability to develop and apply new and innovative ideas and practices . . . . ① ② ③ ④ ⑤

7. TECHNICAL COMPETENCY: The ability to keep current technically and perform his/her work in a knowledgeable manner . . . . ① ② ③ ④ ⑤

8. COMMUNICATING: The ability to express oneself and listen effectively to others . . . . ① ② ③ ④ ⑤

9. DIVERSITY: The willingness to work with diverse individuals and integrate the differences that exist among others . . . . ① ② ③ ④ ⑤

10. TEAM WORK: The ability to work effectively with others towards achieving a common goal . . . . ① ② ③ ④ ⑤

11. MENTORING: The willingness to help others acquire the knowledge and skills necessary for their personal and professional development . . . . ① ② ③ ④ ⑤

> **Please try to use each of the five (5) columns as you rate the importance of each skill.**

69

Part B. Professional Skills and Practices

■ As you think about the person who sent you this survey, indicate **how often** this person currently performs the skill or practice now (**Current Performance**) and **how often you expect** these same practices to occur (**Your Expectations**).

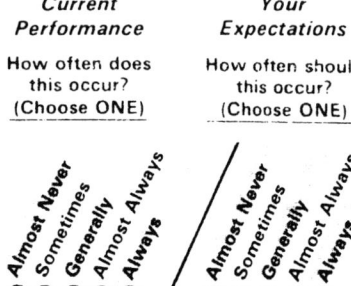

Current Performance

How often does this occur? (Choose ONE)

Your Expectations

How often should this occur? (Choose ONE)

Be sure to complete both columns

■ This is not a test.

■ There are no right or wrong answers.

■ 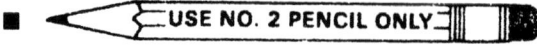 USE NO. 2 PENCIL ONLY

■ **Note:** With the exception of the "Boss," all responses will be kept strictly confidential.

■ *If you are the person who sent these surveys to others, assess your own professional skills and practices.*

Skip any item if you feel you cannot make an accurate assessment.

	Current Performance	Your Expectations
	How often does this occur? (Choose ONE)	How often should this occur? (Choose ONE)

Please complete each item based on your observation of, and interaction with, the person who sent you this survey.

To what extent does this person . . .

1. Set high standards for her/his work performance? .... ① ② ③ ④ ⑤   ① ② ③ ④ ⑤

2. Seek responsibilities beyond his/her job description? .... ① ② ③ ④ ⑤   ① ② ③ ④ ⑤

3. Generate alternative solutions when resolving problems? .... ① ② ③ ④ ⑤   ① ② ③ ④ ⑤

4. Develop practical methods for implementing creative ideas? .... ① ② ③ ④ ⑤   ① ② ③ ④ ⑤

5. Express his/her point of view in a tactful way? .... ① ② ③ ④ ⑤   ① ② ③ ④ ⑤

6. Appear to be approachable and easy to talk with? .... ① ② ③ ④ ⑤   ① ② ③ ④ ⑤

7. Work hard to satisfy customer (internal or external) requirements? .... ① ② ③ ④ ⑤   ① ② ③ ④ ⑤

8. Complete tasks, projects within the allocated budget? .... ① ② ③ ④ ⑤   ① ② ③ ④ ⑤

9. Demonstrate technical competence when working with you/others? .... ① ② ③ ④ ⑤   ① ② ③ ④ ⑤

10. Write in a clear and concise style? .... ① ② ③ ④ ⑤   ① ② ③ ④ ⑤

Be sure to complete both columns

Case Study

HUMAN FACTORS INTERNATIONAL

Professional Management Style Questionnaire for A.N. Other

Organising

■ - *You*   ■ - *Your boss*   ■ - *Your Peers*   ■ - *Your subordinates*

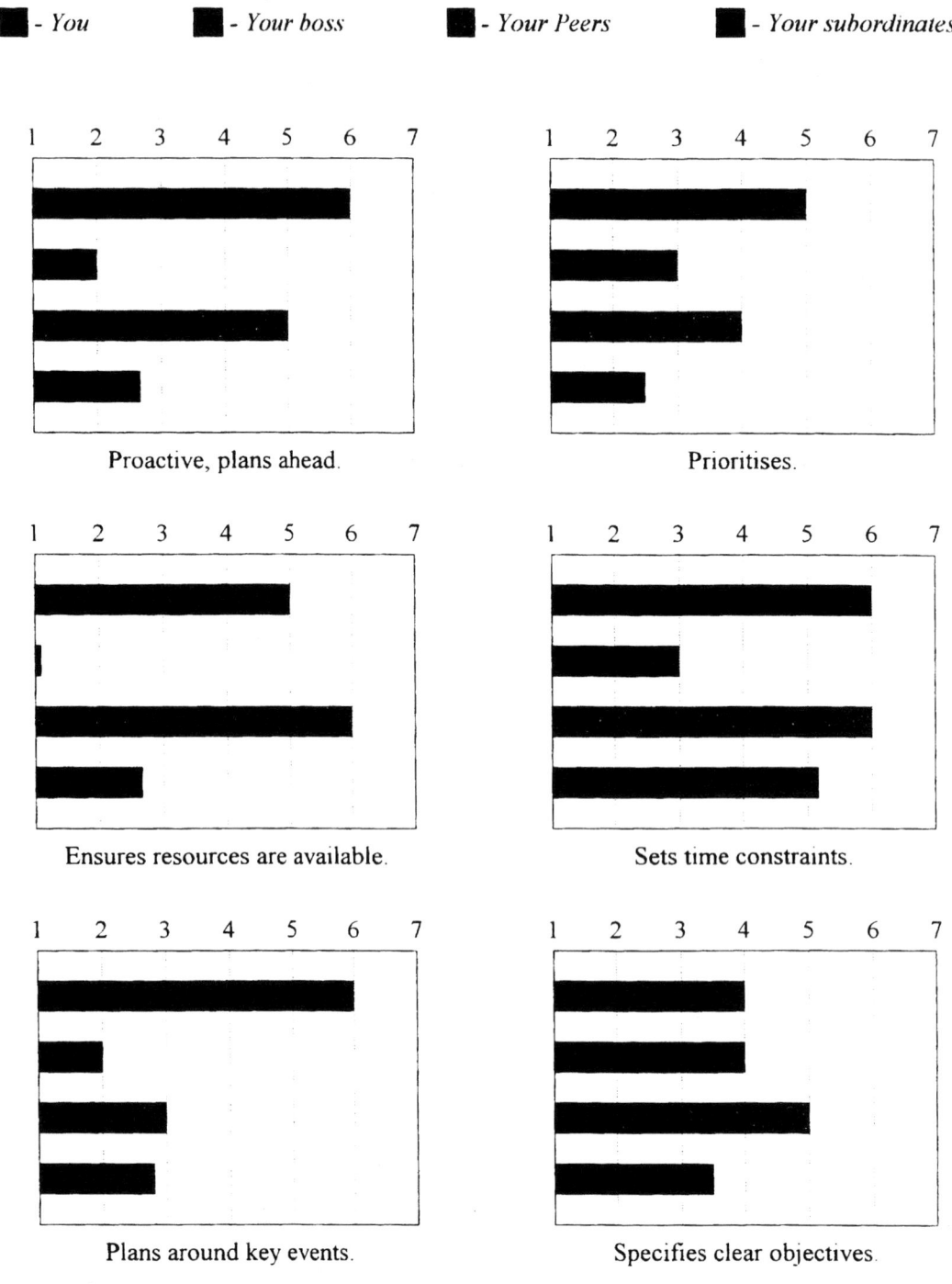

Proactive, plans ahead.

Prioritises.

Ensures resources are available.

Sets time constraints.

Plans around key events.

Specifies clear objectives.

1 - 3 : Poor   3 - 5 : Good   5 - 7 : Excellent

Human Factors International   Eastone Hall, Stratford Road, Henley-in-Arden, West Midlands B95 6DD
Telephone: 01926 843717   Fax: 01926 843727

Professional Management Style Questionnaire for A.N. Other

Development Needs

■ - *You*   ■ - *Your boss*   ■ - *Your Peers*   ■ - *Your subordinates*

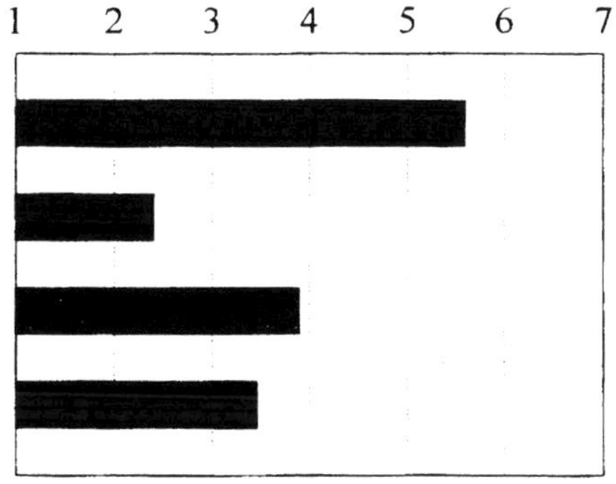

Management Function.

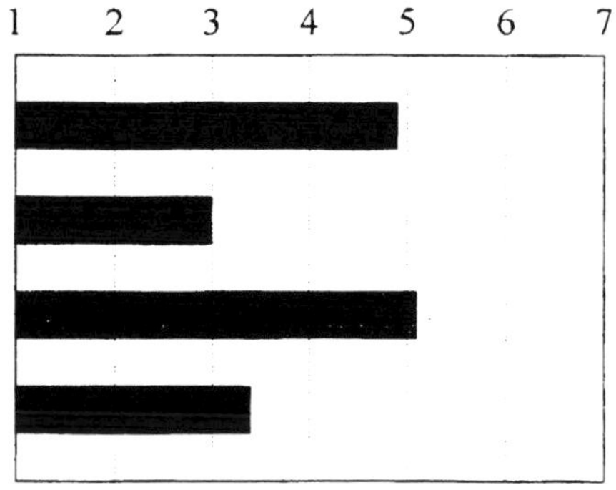

Decision Making.

Personal Resourcefulness.

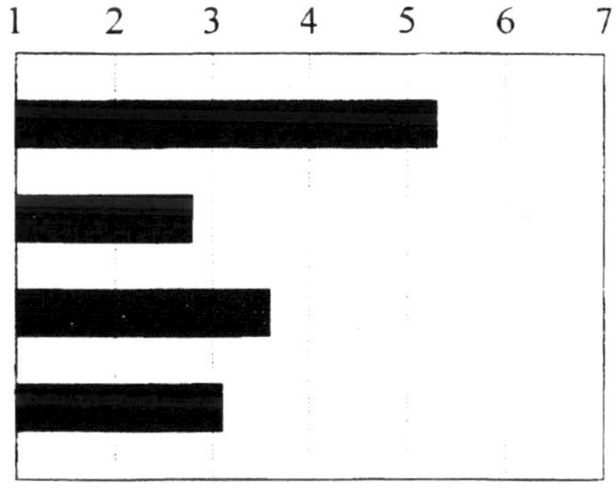

Performance Management.

Management Style.

Teamwork.

1 - 3 : Poor   3 - 5 : Good   5 - 7 : Excellent

Human Factors International   Edstone Hall, Stratford Road, Henley-in-Arden, West Midlands B95 6DD
Telephone: 01926 843717 Fax: 01926 843727

Case Study

MERCURY COMMUNICATIONS

Contributor: HR Manager, Training and Development

Mercury Communications is a relatively young telecommunications company, formed in the early 1980s as the original competitor to BT. Mercury is predominantly owned by Cable and Wireless plc which itself operates in over forty countries through a complex web of wholly owned businesses, joint ventures and equity interests. Mercury introduced 360 degree review as part of its new performance and development system, Contribution Management. Andy Gillham, then the HR Director of its Enterprise Business Unit, joined a multi-disciplinary team led by the Employee Relations Manager and taken from across the organisation to specify, design and launch the system.

> In 1993, we needed to review our existing appraisal system. As a young but complex company, we tend to be quite innovative and change oriented and it was important that whatever we designed would be relevant to the whole business and stand the test of time. We reviewed what the market was doing and benchmarked best practice.
>
> We found that other systems had their strengths and weaknesses but elected to create a process that was quite different, comprising a number of discrete tools including 360 review. We determined that any value that 360 degree appraisal added to the business would lie in the quality of its application but that it represented the most direct indicator of performance available to us. 360 degreee appraisal now sits within the Contribution Management system as one of a number of discretionary tools accessible by all employees via a network of servers.
>
> The 360 degree review is a simple tool but is designed to be used in conjunction with the organisation's competency framework providing a structure within which performance and development discussions can be held.
>
> Three years after its introduction, 360 degree appraisal is also being used, not only within Contribution Management, but also as a major element of the company's General Assessment process. Significantly it is becoming part and parcel of the language of the business, indicating that it is getting embedded into the way Mercury manages its employees. This is a significant step in a business where, historically, policies and procedures have tended not to remain in place long

enough for them to become a habit. We monitor Contribution Management and over 90% of employees use the system, with 360 degree appraisal being used increasingly in these discussions.

360 degree appraisal is used very pragmatically. The data supports a number of related processes including Succession Planning and Personal Development Planning. We find that managers are able to manage the process and if an individual tries to abuse the system it is transparent enough for them to pick this up.

C O N T R I B U T I O N   M A N A G E M E N T

360º Feedback planner			
I will seek feedback from the following:			
Names	**Position**	**Given form/date**	**Discussed/date**
Managers			
* _____	* _____		
* _____	* _____		
* _____	* _____		
Peers/Team Members			
* _____	* _____		
* _____	* _____		
* _____	* _____		
Reports			
* _____	* _____		
* _____	* _____		
* _____	* _____		
Customers			
* _____	* _____		
* _____	* _____		
* _____	* _____		

Contribution Management - 360 Feedback

C O N T R I B U T I O N   M A N A G E M E N T

360° Feedback form

Please use this form to prepare for a feedback meeting with me fixed for:

Day: _____ Date: _____ Time: _____

THIS FORM IS CONFIDENTIAL AND WILL ONLY BE SEEN BY YOU AND ME

Giver of feedback: _____ Receiver: _____ Review Period: _____

List here 3 specific examples of things I do well
Example 1
Example 2
Example 3

List here 3 specific examples of things I should do better
Example 1
Example 2
Example 3

Contribution Management - 360 Feedback

C O N T R I B U T I O N   M A N A G E M E N T

360° Feedback summary	
Following the feedback I have received my three most important strengths are:	
Strengths	**Opportunities to exploit**
1	
2	
3	

Contribution Management - 360 Feedback

Case Study

KERR BROWN PDI

(sample pages from self-assessment questionnaire)

PROFILOR

Developmental Feedback for Managers

QUESTIONNAIRE

	To a Very Great Extent	To a Great Extent	To Some Extent	To a Little Extent	Not At All	Does Not Apply
You:						
42. Give specific and constructive feedback	5	4	3	2	1	N
43. Convey trust in people's competence to do their jobs	5	4	3	2	1	N
44. Involve others in shaping plans and decisions that affect them	5	4	3	2	1	N
45. Confront problems early, before they get out of hand	5	4	3	2	1	N
46. Live up to commitments	5	4	3	2	1	N
47. Are flexible	5	4	3	2	1	N
48. Adapt behaviour in response to feedback and experience	5	4	3	2	1	N
49. Seek out new work challenges	5	4	3	2	1	N
50. Stimulate others to make changes and improvements	5	4	3	2	1	N
51. Get work done on time	5	4	3	2	1	N
52. Know when to supervise and coach people and when to leave them on their own	5	4	3	2	1	N
53. Prepare realistic estimates of budget, staff, and other resources	5	4	3	2	1	N
54. Delegate assignments to the lowest appropriate level	5	4	3	2	1	N
55. Can be approached easily	5	4	3	2	1	N
56. Anticipate the positions and reactions of others accurately	5	4	3	2	1	N
57. Work toward win/win solutions whenever possible	5	4	3	2	1	N
58. Understand complex concepts and relationships	5	4	3	2	1	N
59. Keep up to date on professional/technical developments	5	4	3	2	1	N
60. Understand the organisation's mission, strategies, strengths, and weaknesses	5	4	3	2	1	N
61. Get point across when talking	5	4	3	2	1	N
62. Keep people up to date with information	5	4	3	2	1	N
63. Listen to people without interrupting	5	4	3	2	1	N
64. Give persuasive reasons for ideas	5	4	3	2	1	N
65. Clarify roles and responsibilities with team members	5	4	3	2	1	N
66. Let people know when they are performing well	5	4	3	2	1	N
67. Inspire people to excel	5	4	3	2	1	N
68. Use a team approach to solve problems when appropriate	5	4	3	2	1	N
69. Challenge others to make tough choices	5	4	3	2	1	N
70. Encourage discussion of ethical considerations before decisions are made	5	4	3	2	1	N
71. Work constructively under stress and pressure	5	4	3	2	1	N
72. Initiate activities without being asked to do so	5	4	3	2	1	N
73. Pursue learning and self-development	5	4	3	2	1	N
74. Involve others in the change process	5	4	3	2	1	N
75. Accomplish a great deal	5	4	3	2	1	N
76. Anticipate problems and develop contingency plans	5	4	3	2	1	N
77. Give people the latitude to manage their own responsibilities	5	4	3	2	1	N
78. Develop effective working relationships with direct reports	5	4	3	2	1	N
79. Compromise to build give-and-take relationships with others	5	4	3	2	1	N
80. Focus on important information without getting bogged down in unnecessary detail	5	4	3	2	1	N
81. Present technical information in easily understood terms	5	4	3	2	1	N

PROFİLOR

Developmental Feedback for Managers

QUESTIONNAIRE

	To a Very Great Extent	To a Great Extent	To Some Extent	To a Little Extent	Not At All	Does Not Apply
You:						
82. Understand how the business is run	5	4	3	2	1	N
83. Speak effectively in front of a group	5	4	3	2	1	N
84. Create an environment where people work their best	5	4	3	2	1	N
85. Clarify what people say to ensure understanding	5	4	3	2	1	N
86. Are assertive	5	4	3	2	1	N
87. Provide others with open access to information	5	4	3	2	1	N
88. Link the team's mission to that of the broader organisation	5	4	3	2	1	N
89. Let people know when results are not up to expectations	5	4	3	2	1	N
90. Create an environment that makes work enjoyable	5	4	3	2	1	N
91. Foster teamwork within the team	5	4	3	2	1	N
92. Drive hard on the right issues	5	4	3	2	1	N
93. Protect confidential information	5	4	3	2	1	N
94. Work effectively in ambiguous situations	5	4	3	2	1	N
95. Convey a sense of urgency when appropriate	5	4	3	2	1	N
96. Prepare people to understand changes	5	4	3	2	1	N
97. Are an effective manager overall	5	4	3	2	1	N
98. Set up needed systems and structures to support changes	5	4	3	2	1	N
99. Produce high quality work	5	4	3	2	1	N
100. Integrate planning efforts across work units	5	4	3	2	1	N
101. Give others the authority necessary to accomplish their objectives	5	4	3	2	1	N
102. Are accessible to provide assistance/support as necessary	5	4	3	2	1	N
103. Monitor progress of others and redirect efforts when goals are not being met	5	4	3	2	1	N
104. Develop effective working relationships with colleagues	5	4	3	2	1	N
105. Listen carefully to input	5	4	3	2	1	N
106. Bring cross-disciplinary knowledge to bear on issues and opportunities	5	4	3	2	1	N
107. Apply logic in solving problems	5	4	3	2	1	N
108. Make sure that people have no "surprises"	5	4	3	2	1	N
109. Listen willingly to concerns expressed by others	5	4	3	2	1	N
110. Win support from others	5	4	3	2	1	N
111. Get others to take action	5	4	3	2	1	N
112. Make the team mission and strategies clear to others	5	4	3	2	1	N
113. Make decisions in the face of uncertainty	5	4	3	2	1	N
114. Reward people for good performance	5	4	3	2	1	N
115. Promote teamwork among groups; discourage "we vs. they" thinking	5	4	3	2	1	N
116. Act decisively	5	4	3	2	1	N
117. Coach others in the development of their skills	5	4	3	2	1	N
118. Adapt approach to motivate each individual	5	4	3	2	1	N
119. Acknowledge and celebrate team accomplishments	5	4	3	2	1	N
120. Demonstrate managerial courage	5	4	3	2	1	N
121. Provide challenging assignments to facilitate individual development	5	4	3	2	1	N

PROFILOR

Developmental Feedback for Managers

QUESTIONNAIRE

	Critically Important (no more than 8)	Very Important (no more than 8)	Important

13. **Display Organisational Savvy:** Develops effective give-and-take relationships with others; understands the agendas and perspectives of others; recognises and effectively balances the interests and needs of one's own group with those of the broader organisation....................... 7 6   5 4 3   2 1

14. **Manage Disagreements:** Brings substantive conflicts and disagreements into the open and attempts to resolve them collaboratively; builds consensus 7 6   5 4 3   2 1

15. **Speak Effectively:** Speaks clearly and expresses self well in groups and in one-to-one conversations 7 6   5 4 3   2 1

16. **Foster Open Communication:** Creates an atmosphere in which timely and high quality information flows smoothly between self and others; encourages the open expression of ideas and opinions 7 6   5 4 3   2 1

17. **Listen to Others:** Demonstrates attention to and conveys understanding of the comments and questions of others; listens well in a group 7 6   5 4 3   2 1

18. **Drive for Results:** Drives for results and success; conveys a sense of urgency and drives issues to conclusions; persists despite obstacles and opposition 7 6   5 4 3   2 1

19. **Show Work Commitment:** Sets high standards of performance; pursues challenging goals and works hard to achieve them 7 6   5 4 3   2 1

20. **Act with Integrity:** Demonstrates principled leadership and sound business ethics; shows consistency among principles, values, and behaviour; builds trust with others through own authenticity and follow-through on commitments............. 7 6   5 4 3   2 1

21. **Demonstrate Adaptability:** Handles day-to-day work challenges confidently; is willing and able to adjust to multiple demands, shifting priorities, ambiguity, and rapid change; shows resilience in the face of constraints, frustrations, or adversity; demonstrates flexibility......................... 7 6   5 4 3   2 1

22. **Develop Oneself:** Learns from experience; actively pursues learning and self-development; seeks feedback and welcomes unsolicited feedback; modifies behaviour in light of feedback......................... 7 6   5 4 3   2 1

23. **Use Technical/Functional Expertise:** Possesses up to date knowledge in the profession and industry; is regarded as an expert in the technical/functional area; accesses and uses other expert resources when appropriate....................... 7 6   5 4 3   2 1

24. **Know the Business:** Shows understanding of issues relevant to the broad organisation and business; keeps that knowledge up to date; has and uses knowledge from different areas 7 6   5 4 3   2 1

Case Study

WARNER BURKE ASSOCIATES

Managerial Self-Awareness: in High Performing Individuals in Organisations

Allan H. Church, PhD
W. Warner Burke Associates, Inc.
201 Wolfs Lane, Pelham, NY 10803 USA
Telephone (914) 738-0080
Facsimile (914) 738-1059

AllanHC @ AOL.COM

Summary

Agreement or congruence between an individual manager's self ratings on an assessment instrument and those obtained from a variety of other sources in the workplace (e.g. direct reports, peers, supervisors, suppliers, clients) has become a primary indicator of an individual's level of managerial self-awareness. Conceptualised as both a personality trait and as a learned skill or ability, this construct is likely to interact with the perception process prior to self-assessment which, in turn, moderates the self-other rating comparison. Managerial self-awareness (MSA) is defined as the ability to reflect on and accurately assess one's own behaviours and skills as they are manifested in workplace interactions. Practitioners in the field of organisation change and development have been operating according to the principle of enhancing self-awareness through database methods for years. It is an important assumption of many leadership and management training and development programmes that if a manager is to be maximally effective, he or she must be made aware of (a) his or her own actions and (b) the consequences of those actions on others through some form of individually directed feedback process. Such belief is also reflected in the ever increasing popularity of multirater or 360 degree feedback systems for managerial assessment and development purposes.

The following study examined empirically the relationship between congruence or agreement in self versus others' ratings – believed to reflect an individual's level of managerial self-awareness – and individual performance. Data were collected from 134 high performing (HPs) and 470 average performing (AVs) middle and senior level managers and their direct reports from three different organisations and industries: technological, pharmaceutical and an airline service. In total, high performers (HPs) were rated by 973 direct reports and average performers (AVs) by 3,398 direct reports. Behaviour ratings and demographic information were obtained from managers and their staff prior to their attending a feedback-based management development programme. Analyses were based on the overall level of agreement in self versus direct reports' average ratings. High performers from these organisations were identified by several different means including external assessments based on case histories of each manager, number of meritorious awards and promotions received, selection into a high potential senior executive development programme, and identification by the senior-most managers in the organisation as being high performers.

Results of the study indicated that high performers were significantly more managerially self-aware – and thereby demonstrated greater congruence in self versus others' ratings – compared with average performers. This relationship was true regardless of the organisational setting or the method for assessing performance. Thus, high performing managers were able to assess more accurately their own behaviours in the workplace, yielding greater congruence in self versus direct reports' ratings, compared with average performers. Interestingly, no overall relationships were found between congruence and gender, age or tenure. As in previous research, there was a general tendency on the part of managers to rate themselves somewhat higher across all behaviours than did their direct reports.

5 Evaluation

'With any new initiative, as soon as things get difficult people will disown the new method as coming from the outside, head office, or whatever, and pretend it is absolutely nothing to do with them.'

Searching for the right solution is what you will continue to strive to do after the consultant's fees have been paid and you have left the organisation. Sounds strange, but sorry to disappoint you, nobody ever gets it perfect so that it cannot be improved upon. It would be nice if that were possible, but as people, companies and markets are constantly changing, development needs will also change.

360 degree appraisal can certainly be used to leverage change and will move forward with the company, but please don't think that it is the only solution you will ever need. For it to be used effectively 360 degree appraisal needs to be linked with other initiatives to provide a development framework for the organisation.

This report will provide some guidance as to how to source specialist assistance. If you are in any doubt about professional standards, contact the Institute of Personnel and Development or the British Psychological Society.

5.1 Paper and Pencil vs Screen Administered

Evaluation of processes such as 360 degree appraisal is part of the cycle which will assist you to refine and change your methodology to make it more effective. This means that you and your organisation will become more effective, more able to compete and more responsive after successful implementation.

One major issue concerning evaluation is how much technology to involve in the process. This is because the main hindrance and problem with the implementation of developmental processes is time. If you can plan and design how you will introduce 360 degree appraisal with real precision, taking into account logistics and resources, you will succeed.

There are many 'expert' systems now available and you will find that some of them are straightforward databases which look very impressive and others are based on more complex modelling. The statistical precision and expertise necessary to write good software remains in the domain of the specialist. These types of systems will allow professional administration and interpretation of questionnaires.

Since the origins of testing, people have been concerned with the drive towards objectivity and scientific approaches. The personal computer has enabled occupational psychologists to create more distance between themselves and their candidates.

In the US, Sam Krug's company (Metritech) surveyed 329 users of computer-assisted narrative reports who used a variety of tests and found the quality and availability of documentation to support the materials were significant to the satisfaction of users of such instruments. Research by both Skinner and Allen (1983) and Harrell and Lombardi (1984) all found that people being tested preferred the computer to a human or paper and pencil interrogator. In the UK many test publishers have discovered clients do prefer computer scoring and printing for a variety of reasons including speed, confidentiality and consistency.

5.2   Various Consequences of Implementation

Nobody can really fully predict all associated consequences. However, your job or that of the consultants you employ is to make reasoned predictions of positive outcomes and to be aware of how to avoid negative outcomes.

5.3   Some Barriers to Implementation

- It may be difficult to arrange time to bring managers together for full briefings.

- People will miss deadlines and lose questionnaires.

- A few employees become difficult and refuse to co-operate.

- A superior performer emerges and asks for a large wage increase.

- An individual finds the feedback difficult to handle.

Although this presents a negative picture, it is important you realise without sufficient preparation any of the above and more could occur. If you prepare and plan with precision, the picture could look like this:

- Top 50 managers adopt 360 degree appraisal.

- Next 150 participate.

- All employees paid between £15,000 and £25,000 are next.

- People in the organisation decide to include suppliers.

- A number of customers agree to participate.

It is probable that some individuals will react with surprise when their results are produced. Please remember, this may be the first time an individual has thought about their personal qualities to this degree and if you really want to introduce 360 degree appraisal to assist in improving individual and team performance, you must expect some degree of discomfort.

5.4 The Moment of Truth

This is probably where the most important part of the process will occur. This is the 'moment of truth' with 360 degree appraisal, the time when the gap in perception is uncovered. The collective subjectivity of a number of respondents will provide a rating of an individual's performance at work. The individual will also provide a rating. It is the difference in how people rate themselves and how other people rate them which is of most interest. What is also critical is how the feedback process is managed in terms of people accepting the ratings.

Until this is an established practice at every level of your organisation, you must ensure that an appropriately trained individual manages this part of the process with sensitivity. If you do not, the real value of 360 degree appraisal will not be achieved.

5.5 Is Feedback Such a New Idea?

It depends on which expert you speak with. Dr Joyce Willard of Forum Europe (a leading supplier of 360 degree products and systems) speaks of 360 degree appraisal and draws parallels between the feedback content of 360 degree processes and the relationship between a 'mentor' and an 'apprentice.'

So, for example, imagine a piece of furniture at a market stall and a customer is trying to decide whether the price is right. Naturally, thoughts and opinions may occur such as, 'Is it well made?' or 'Is the design in keeping with the taste of my family and friends?' You may well imagine the discussion between master and craftsperson after the customer walked away without purchasing this delightful piece which took all of an age and a day to make. The discussion might be to apportion 'blame' as to why the customer did not part with their hard earned cash.

The master may conclude that the apprentice did not listen intently to the messages given during the instructional process. Messages such as 'You are so undisciplined, you are never on time and you must watch what I am doing much more carefully in future.' The apprentice may say in his or her defence 'You did not make clear what was required of me' or 'Our products are out of date and our customers can see that.'

For master, substitute head of international group and for apprentice, substitute managing director of its least profitable trading company employing 7,500 people.

Let's move forward in time and take a look at a large conglomerate which had as many layers of management as floors in the building. At this point, try to imagine dusting off the cobwebs of what now seems an ancient management structure and transform it into a busy, thriving modern office with the latest technology and thinking.

The ever elusive search for the 'holy grail' or best practice in HRD (Human Resource Development) has challenged thinking and practices within the education and training industry so that many firms are now looking at staff development from the simpler perspective of 'How can this individual make more money or prove they are genuinely more productive than they were last year?'

Therefore, 'shareholder value' has emerged as a concept for personnel to really embrace. If your organisation is not publicly quoted, there will naturally be differences; however, the trend is generally towards improvement in the performance of staff at all levels and to ignore proven methods of staff development is a financial issue.

Sir Francis Bacon: 'In nature, things move violently to their place and calmly in their place.'

5.6   Measurement and Control

Your measurement and control systems will need to adapt to any changes in order to assess the increases in performance from either a human or a financial perspective. There are numerous examples of how more rigorous selection methods have saved money. One classic example was with a security firm which was experiencing problems recruiting in urban areas. The firm employed a leading consulting firm to design a new recruitment procedure based on a specific personality measure and biographical data which was presented to candidates as a computer questionnaire.

This documented case study showed savings of over £250,000 in its first year of use (1990) and this was with only partial implementation. The new recruitment system reduced considerably the time taken to select people who were within the criteria identified for people who would perform well and stay with the company. This case study clearly illustrated how professional psychology may be used to address a business problem. The organisation saved money in terms of:

- reduced staff turnover;

- less time spent in face to face interviewing;

- more committed personnel;

- better team-workers;

- more responsible employees.

The company knew they were having difficulty with staff recruitment and retention and they also knew they needed assistance. They worked in collaboration with the consulting firm and developed a new approach. The consulting firm jointly designed the evaluation project. The consultants 'closed the loop' and established value financially. The company had less problems with more profits and employees experienced less stress and were better able to cope with the job. Therefore shareholder value was increased.

This case study is representative of good practice. The simple rules of 'contracting' were followed and the results are documented financially.

The mistake which could have been made was for the consultants to have completed the task and not spent so much time on evaluation. It happens all too frequently and both consultants and companies are unaware of the true value of their efforts. This is a critical area for 360 degree appraisal as the evaluation may be short, medium or long term. You must decide how this is to be achieved and which performance indicators will be used to plot success or failure.

5.7   Beyond Competencies, Thinking Globally

Around a billion people, from an approximate population of 6 billion, are able to communicate readily and easily from country to country and this presents some good challenges ahead in terms of the assessment of people within the framework of globalisation. Multilingual assessments will become more common and as new behaviours develop, we will probably see a continuing change in people process development.

The Asea Brown Boveri Group was born of a merger between ASEA AB, Stockholm and BBC Brown Boveri Ltd, Baden, Switzerland. Anders Lidefelt, head of capital markets at ABB International has described ABB as 'multi-domestic' rather than a 'multi-national' company. It includes over 1,300 companies, 50 business areas, has 207,557 employees and US$ 31 billion in orders received (December 1995).

There is research from a leading British business school that has looked at the behaviours associated with success in an international environment which concludes that:

> Successful people appear to be operating from a deeper, core competence which is essentially holistic. This is described as having three major interlinking parts: cognitive complexity, emotional energy and psychological maturity.

360 degree appraisal will assist in developing people for international careers but the complex planning, modelling and integration required means it is prohibitive in terms of costs for less profitable companies. Many of the world's leading airlines and banks have found systematic methods for evaluating their training and you may notice how particular awards are given in industry for 'best practice'. The challenge is now for a British firm to become recognised by a leading institute as best practitioners in terms of 360 degree development. Only then will we be able to begin to establish essential 'codes of practice' plus a qualification route which will ensure we develop people to perform at their best, without compromising on standards.

Endnote

This report has been written to assist 'best practice' at work. 360 degree appraisal may be used to select future business leaders, senior managers or to confirm who is worthy of promotion. If used by the untrained, it can lead to problems which cause difficulties at work which will be costly to remedy. If 360 processes are not managed by professionals, it could be the cause of mistrust leading to conflict and confusion.

However, if it is well positioned as an organisational process, with good support and guidance, it becomes a powerful assessment solution.

Recent surveys indicate that a number of leading UK organisations have experienced positive and successful outcomes with 360. Most are planning to expand its use and the vast majority of managers find the process useful. 360 is becoming embedded into the culture of many successful companies to give a competitive edge and to increase service and response. If you decide to implement this powerful assessment method, you are recommended to seek professional assistance.

References

BOYATZIS, R.E. (1982). *The Competent Manager: Model for Effective Performance*, Wiley.

CATTEL, R.B., EBER, H.W. and TATSOUKA, M.M. (1970). *Handbook for the Sixteen Personality Factor Questionnaire*, Institute for Personality and Ability Testing, Lacy Champaign, Illinois.

DEMING, W.E. (1986). *Out of the Crisis.* Cambridge, MA: MIT, Centre for Advanced Engineering Study.

GANNON, M. (1995) *The Performance Management Handbook.* Institute of Personnel and Development.

HARRELL, T.H. and LOMBARDI, T.A. (1984). Validation of an Automated 16PF Administration Procedure. *Journal of Personality Assessment,* Vol. 48, pp. 638-642.

IMPARATO, N. and HARARI, O. (1994) *Jumping the Curve. Innovation and Strategic Choice in an Age of Transition.* Jossey-Bass, San Francisco.

KEMPTON, J. (1995) *Human Resource Management and Development. Current Issues and Themes.* Macmillan Press Ltd.

KRUG, S.E. (1990). Paper presented at APA Convention, Boston, USA.

MYERS, I.B. and McCAULLEY, M.H. (1985). *Manual: A Guide to the Development and Use of the Myers-Briggs Type Indicator.* Consulting Psychologists Press, Inc., Palo Alto, California.

SELBY, C. (1992). *Personnel Assessment - The Impact of Computers.* International Test Commission Bulletin, Vol. 19, No. 1. Presented at the 2nd European Congress of Psychology Budapest 1991.

SHACKELTON, V. and NEWELL, S. (1991). Management Selection: A Comparative Survey of Methods Used in Top British and French Companies. *Journal of Occupational Psychology,* Vol. 64.

SKINNER, H.A. and ALLEN, B.A. (1983). Does the Computer Make a Difference? Computerised Versus Face-to-Face Self-Report Assessment of Alcohol, Drug and Tobacco Use. *Journal of Consulting and Clinical Psychology,* Vol. 51, pp. 267-275.

SMITH, M. (1988). Selection: Where Are The Best Prophets? *Personnel Management*, December.

THATCHER, M. (1995). *Investors Chronicle*, Vol. 113, p. 1442.

TISDALL, P. (1982) *Agents of Change. The Development and Practice of Management Consultancy.* Heinemann, London.

WALTER, N. (1995). Association of Outplacement Consulting Firms International Conference, London.

Useful addresses

The British Psychological Society
St. Andrews House
48, Princess Road East
Leicester
LE1 7DR

The Institute of Personnel and Development
IPD House
Camp Road
London
SW19 4UX